Town Nyanja

A learner's guide to Zambia's emerging national language

Andrew Gray, Brighton Lubasi & Phallen Bwalya

Copyright © 2013 by Andrew Gray, Brighton Lubasi and Phallen Bwalya.

All rights reserved. No part of this publication may be reproduced, stored or introduced into a retrieval system, or transmitted, in any form or by any means (electronic, mechanical, photocopying, recording or otherwise), without the prior written permission of the authors.

ISBN 978-1-300-75600-2

Contents

Introduction	5
Sounds and spellings	6
Grammar	10
Nouns	10
Verbs	18
Pronouns	25
Describing things	27
Instructions	28
Questions	29
Conjunctions	30
Useful phrases	**31**
Basics	31
Describing people	32
Getting around	33
Accommodation	35
Shopping	36
Dining	37
Work and business	38
Social / household	39
Emergencies	40
English-Nyanja vocabulary	41
Nyanja-English vocabulary	61

Acknowledgements

Many thanks to Alastair Cole, Kylie Hutchinson, Cynthia Moeller and others who have provided helpful comments and input into this book.

This book has been inspired by the iSchool interactive learning project, a pioneer in the production of modern educational materials in Zambian languages. If you are interested in reading more in Town Nyanja, visit www.ischool.zm

If you have any feedback on this book, please email nyanja@andrewgray.com

Introduction

The common language used on the streets of Lusaka is a form of Nyanja, the "language of the lake" traditionally spoken in the east of Zambia and in neighbouring Malawi (where it is known as Chewa). However, any visitor arriving in the Zambian capital today with a dictionary or phrasebook of standard Nyanja will find it virtually useless. In the century since Lusaka was settled, new expressions have been invented, old ones have dropped out of use, features that once belonged to local dialects such as Nsenga have become widespread, and the language has absorbed words on a massive scale, most noticeably from English but also from Bemba and the many other Zambian languages whose speakers congregate in Lusaka.

With its local roots, this new language flows more easily off the tongues of Lusaka's residents than the English that is taught in school. Although English remains the language of officialdom and business, and of the educated upper classes, it is in Nyanja that ordinary people on the street most commonly communicate. Through migration and the media, this new 'Town Nyanja' has also spread beyond Lusaka to other areas where Zambians find themselves in need of a common local language.

Despite being the lingua franca of a city of a million and a half people, and the closest thing Zambia has to an indigenous national language, no books have been written in Town Nyanja, and the language has no official status. Many dismiss it as little more than slang, or as an 'incorrect' form which threatens the purity of Zambia's established languages. Even educators who do value Town Nyanja often claim that it is too varied and rapidly-changing to be worth writing down.

Town Nyanja is indeed diverse and evolving, like any living language. However, as this book shows, the language does have a core vocabulary and grammar which is consistent and structured, but different from that of standard Nyanja. And groups producing written materials for a mass audience in Zambia, such as the iSchool interactive learning project, are increasingly finding that they do need to try and write in Town Nyanja, since modern urban readers simply don't understand Nyanja in its standard form.

Proper linguistic study into Town Nyanja is urgently needed, followed by discussion and agreement on how to write the language down. This book represents only a small step in this process. However, we hope it will help visitors to urban Zambia to learn the language spoken there, instead of mangling and denigrating it because it happens to be different from the language of rural Eastern province. Perhaps it will also provide future Zambian historians with a record of a stage in the development of a true national language.

Sounds and spellings

The range of sounds used in Town Nyanja, and the letters used to represent them, are shown below. This is somewhat different from the range of sounds found in standard Nyanja (shown alongside for comparison), although people writing Town Nyanja are often influenced by standard Nyanja spellings.

		As in Town Nyanja	Approximately like in English	Standard Nyanja equivalents
a		nd<u>a</u>l<u>a</u>m<u>a</u> "money"	f<u>a</u>ther	a
b	- hard	-<u>b</u>wela "come"	<u>b</u>ank	b
	- soft (β)	<u>β</u>ana "children"	—	ŵ
ch		<u>ch</u>intu "thing"	<u>ch</u>op	c, ch
d		<u>d</u>oti "rubbish"	<u>d</u>og	d
e		m<u>e</u>nso "eyes"	wh<u>e</u>re	e
f		-<u>f</u>ika "arrive"	<u>f</u>oot	f, pf
g		-<u>g</u>wila "touch"	<u>g</u>irl	g
h		<u>h</u>onda "motorbike"	<u>h</u>ead	h
i		<u>i</u>mbwa "dog"	mar<u>i</u>ne	i
j		-<u>j</u>umpa "jump"	<u>j</u>acket	j
k		<u>k</u>alulu "rabbit"	<u>k</u>ick	k, kh
l		l<u>e</u>lo "today"	<u>l</u>emon	l, r
m		<u>m</u>utu "head"	<u>m</u>an	m
n		<u>n</u>amba "number"	<u>n</u>ose	n
ng'		<u>ng'</u>ombe "cow"	si<u>ng</u>er	ng'
o		<u>o</u>l<u>o</u> "or"	h<u>o</u>le	o
p		<u>p</u>usi "cat"	<u>p</u>ot	p, ph
s		<u>s</u>opo "soap"	<u>s</u>ip	s, ts
sh		-<u>sh</u>eta "chew"	<u>sh</u>eep	—
t		-<u>t</u>andiza "help"	<u>t</u>ap	t, th
u		<u>u</u>sik<u>u</u> "night"	r<u>u</u>de	u
v		<u>v</u>uto "problem"	<u>v</u>an	v, bv
w		-<u>w</u>asha "wash"	<u>w</u>ell	w
y		-<u>y</u>enda "go"	<u>y</u>es	y
z		<u>z</u>ina "name"	<u>z</u>ip	z, dz

Consonants

In Nyanja, as in other Zambian languages, speakers do not distinguish consistently between **l** and **r**. For the sake of consistency, in this book we have used only *l*, except in words borrowed from English. However, in certain words (such as *ndalama* "money") its pronunciation can be *r*-like.

There is a difference between **ng'** (with an apostrophe), which represents a single consonant like in English si*ng*er, and **ng** (without an apostrophe) which represents separate n+g sounds a little like in English fi*ng*er. For native English speakers, pronouncing *ng'* correctly at the start of a word takes practice.

The sound **sh**, which does not occur in standard Nyanja, occurs in Town Nyanja as a result of borrowing from English and from other languages such as Bemba.

A Nyanja sound not found in English is the bilabial fricative, which is pronounced a little like v but with both lips together rather than with the teeth against the lip (or, to describe it another way, like a b sound made without fully closing the lips). In standard Nyanja this sound is written ŵ and in some dialects it is not distinguished from ordinary w, but in Town Nyanja it is generally regarded as a variant of b, as it is in other major Zambian languages such as Bemba. In this book, we have written it using the phonetic symbol β to distinguish it from the English-like *b*, but in everyday writing *b* is used for both sounds. In spoken Town Nyanja, β is distinct both from ordinary *b* and from *w*, as illustrated by the following examples:

<u>w</u>afika? "Did you arrive?" ku<u>β</u>enda "to sneak"
<u>β</u>afika? "Did they arrive?" ku<u>b</u>enda "to bend"

Standard Nyanja has the aspirated consonants **kh**, **ph**, **th** and **ch**, which are distinct from unaspirated *k*, *p*, *t* and *c*. Some dialects also have the affricate consonants **bv**, **pf**, **ts** and **dz**, which are distinct from *v*, *f*, *s* and *z*. These subtle distinctions between consonants, which are not found in most of Zambia's other languages, do not seem to occur consistently in Town Nyanja (though this does not mean to say that the aspirated and affricate consonants are never heard in town), and we have therefore not recognised them in this book.

Vowels

Nyanja has the five standard vowels **a**, **e**, **i**, **o** and **u**.

In standard Nyanja (and other major Zambian languages) there are long vowels – written **aa**, **ee**, **ii**, **oo**, **uu** – which are distinct from their short counterparts. However, pairs of words that show a contrast between long and short vowels are hard to find in Town Nyanja, and we have made very little use of long vowels in this book.

Before vowels the letter **u** becomes **w**, and the letter **i** becomes **y**. For example, the prefix denoting a person (page 10) is normally *mu-* but becomes *mw-* in words like *mwana* "child" (*mu-ana*), and the subject prefix *i-* "it" becomes *y-* in phrases such as *yatyoka* "it's broken" (*i-a-tyoka*).

Contractions

The combination *mu* is commonly shortened to *m'*:

> *mufana* → *m'fana* "younger sibling"
> *mutengo* → *m'tengo* "tree"

-a followed by *ku-* is commonly shortened to *-o-*:

> *nifuna kuziβa* → *nifunoziβa* "I want to know"
> *ananyamuka nakuyenda* → *ananyamuka noyenda* "he got up and went"

In certain cases when a prefix containing *-a* is added to a root beginning with *e-* or *i-*, the vowels combine to make *-e-*. For example, when *mwine* "owner" is pluralised with the prefix *βa*, it forms *βene* "owners" (a contraction of *βa-ine*).

Structure of words

In standard Nyanja, like in most other Zambian languages, words cannot end with a consonant, and groups of consonants such as *bl* and *sp* are mostly forbidden. English words borrowed into standard Nyanja have traditionally been adapted to fit this pattern: for example, "fork" and "spoon" become *foloko* and *supuni*. To some extent this occurs in Town Nyanja too, although many speakers in town pronounce borrowed words like in English, without the extra vowels. For example, a Town Nyanja speaker might say *maket* "market" where a more traditional Nyanja speaker would say *maliketi*. Occasionally speakers will even pronounce native words without the final vowel, for example shortening *bwanji?* "how?" to *bwanj?*.

Where borrowed words are pronounced like in English, speakers generally prefer to see them written like in English too. Educated Zambians are familiar with English spellings, and attempting to spell English words phonetically like in Nyanja (for example, writing *square* as *skwea*) simply causes confusion.

Word division

In deciding how to break phrases up into words, we have largely adhered to the Nyanja orthography rules set down by the Zambia Ministry of Education. In general, Nyanja spellings are quite agglutinative, meaning that they stick small particles together, so a phrase that contains several words in English (such as "You can do it") may be written as one word in Nyanja (*mungaichite*).

The official rules on word division do not cover English-derived words, the use of which is discouraged. In this book, to avoid creating confusing mixed-up words we have always written English words separately from any prefixes and suffixes (*ma words* not **mawords*), regardless of the usual rules.

Tone

Like all Zambian languages, Nyanja is tonal, which means that the meaning of a word or phrase can depend on the way in which the voice rises and falls as the word or phrase is pronounced:

muténgo "tree" (rising & falling tone)
mutengo "price" (flat tone)

ábwela "he's coming" (high tone on first syllable)
abwéla "he has come" (high tone on second syllable)

Intonation (together with differences in the length of vowels) also helps to distinguish Nyanja words and phrases from otherwise-identical equivalents in related languages such as Bemba:

nakana "I refuse" (Nyanja)   *sopo* "soap" (Nyanja)
náakána "I refuse" (Bemba)   *sopó* "soap" (Bemba)

Fortunately, it is nearly always possible to deduce the correct meaning of a word or phrase from the context even if the tone is wrong. Partly for this reason, tone is not usually marked when writing in Zambian languages. However, a foreigner learning Nyanja cannot ignore the fact that native speakers are highly attuned to the tone with which words and phrases are spoken, and those who get their intonation wrong risk being laughed at or not understood. This aspect of the language is difficult to learn from books; learners simply need to try their best to copy the intonation of local speakers.

Grammar

Nouns

Like in all indigenous Zambian languages, and Bantu languages spoken elsewhere in southern Africa, nouns in Nyanja are divided into classes. The way in which nouns form plurals, and the way in which associated words such as "this", "that", "it" and "of" are expressed, depends on which class a noun is in.

In the examples below, the underlined particles (concords) are governed by the class of the noun. The concords differ between the two sentences because *mbuzi* "goats" and *mamotoka* "cars" belong to different noun classes:

> <u>Izi</u> mbuzi <u>zi</u>kulu <u>zi</u>tatu ni <u>za</u>bwino "These three big goats are nice"
> <u>Aya</u> mamotoka <u>ya</u>kulu <u>ya</u>tatu ni <u>ya</u>bwino "These three big cars are nice"

The concords associated with each class are listed on pages 13 and 14. As a rough rule for beginners, when referring to a human the concord is always *u-* or *wa-* (plural *ɓa-*), and for non-humans the safest guess is usually *i-* or *ya-*.

The noun classes are numbered from 1 to 18, following a system that is standard across Bantu languages. The majority of classes come in pairs, with singular and plural forms treated as separate classes (for example, class 2 nouns are the plurals of class 1). The class system of Town Nyanja is based on that of standard Nyanja, detailed descriptions of which can be found in other books, although there are a few differences in prefixes and concords and in the way nouns are classified.

Particular classes of noun have characteristic prefixes and may be loosely associated with particular types of thing – for example, class 7 nouns usually begin with *chi-* and are often names of tools and household objects – but there are no firm rules dictating which class a noun belongs to.

In some cases nouns can be put into a different class by adding or replacing the prefix. For example, class 7 is sometimes associated with big things, and adding the class 7 prefix *chi-* makes something "big" (or, in some contexts, "bad"). Similarly, the class 12 prefix *ka-* makes something "little":

> *nyumba* "house" → *chinyumba* "big house"
> *kanyumba* "little house"

As well as occurring in Nyanja, some of these noun prefixes – in particular, *ɓa-* (respectful), *ma-* (plural), *chi-* (big or bad) and *ka-* (little) – are commonly heard from Zambians speaking English.

The noun classes of Nyanja are summarised below:

Class		Prefix	Examples	Associated with
1	singular	mu- or none	<u>mu</u>ntu "person" <u>mw</u>ana "child"	Humans
2	plural / respectful	βa-	<u>βa</u>ntu "people" <u>βa</u>na "children"	
3	singular	mu-	<u>mu</u>tengo "tree" <u>mu</u>mana "river"	Trees, long or wooden things, natural phenomena
4	plural	mi-	<u>mi</u>tengo "trees" <u>mi</u>mana "rivers"	
5	singular	li- or none	<u>z</u>ina "name" banana "banana"	Miscellaneous nouns including most borrowed words
6	plural / mass noun	ma-	<u>ma</u>zina "names" <u>ma</u>banana "bananas"	
7	singular	chi-	<u>chi</u>ntu "thing" <u>chi</u>pyango "broom"	Tools, household objects, languages, big or bad things
8	plural	vi-	<u>vi</u>ntu "things" <u>vi</u>pyango "brooms"	
9	singular	m-, n-, ng'-	<u>m</u>buzi "goat" <u>n</u>goma "drum"	Some animals, various other nouns
10	plural	same as for singular	<u>m</u>buzi "goats" <u>n</u>goma "drums"	
11	Does not occur as a distinct class in Nyanja			
12	singular	ka-	<u>ka</u>nyoni "(small) bird" <u>ka</u>shimi "(short) story"	Small things
13	plural	tu-	<u>tu</u>nyoni "(small) birds" <u>tu</u>shimi "(short) stories"	
14	abstract / mass noun	u-	<u>u</u>moyo "life" <u>u</u>siku "night"	A few abstracts and mass nouns
15	verbs	ku-	<u>ku</u>penda "counting" <u>ku</u>dya "eating"	Noun forms of verbs (page 18).
16	locative	pa-	<u>pa</u>mwamba "on top"	Locations (page 16).
17		ku-	<u>ku</u>sogolo "at the front"	
18		mu-	<u>mu</u>kati "in the middle"	

Notice that some prefixes are shared by multiple classes: for example, *mu-* is used for class 1 (people), class 3 (trees and long things) and class 18 (interior locations). Also be aware that what looks like a class prefix (such as the *ka-* of *kalulu* "rabbit") may occasionally be part of the noun root instead. To decide what class a noun is in, it is necessary to look at how the noun behaves, not just what prefix it has.

When human beings are being referred to, the concords used are always those of class 1/2 (except when being extremely rude, in which case the class 7/8 prefixes *chi-/vi-* and corresponding concords may be used). This is true even for borrowed nouns pluralised with *ma-* . Thus you can say *magelo ɓoipa* "bad girls" (or in really bad cases *vimagelo voipa*) but not *magelo yoipa. With older people and those in positions of authority, the plural marker *ɓa-* is used as a sign of respect, even if only one person is being referred to. For example, a child would say *ɓatate ɓanga ɓanitandiza*, literally "My fathers help me", in place of "My father helps me".

Words borrowed from English are usually placed in class 5; their plurals are in class 6 and are prefixed with *ma-*. Often the English plural ending *-s* is retained too (*ma guys, ma sweets*). Some educated Zambians disapprove of such 'double plurals' but they are very common in actual speech. The class 6 prefix *ma-* is very widely used in Town Nyanja: in addition to being the usual plural prefix for borrowed words, it also occurs on a large number of native words, including some (such as *manyumba* "houses" and *machule* "frogs") that don't take this prefix in standard Nyanja.

The old class 5 concord *li-*, which has largely disappeared in Town Nyanja, survives in a couple of time-related expressions such as *lionse* "always" and *liti?* "when?" (nouns describing time traditionally belonged to class 5).

In Town Nyanja, singular nouns in class 5 are difficult to distinguish from those in class 9, as they take the same concords (pages 13 and 14), but the corresponding plural forms are distinct. (This situation, in which there are clearer class distinctions among plural nouns than singular ones, is extremely unusual among languages.) Most of the nouns designated in standard Nyanja as 'class 1a' have merged into this class too, and are pluralised with *ma-*, though in some cases the old class 2 plural prefix *ɓa-* is an acceptable alternative (thus "monkeys" may be *makolwe* or *ɓakolwe*).

Some mass nouns, such as *milota* "ashes" (class 4) and *manzi* "water" (class 6), are treated like plurals. These have no singular equivalent.

Class 7/8 concords can be used to refer to 'things' in general (for example, *ichi* "this thing", *vonse* "everything").

Number

The numbers 1-3 are based on the roots -*mozi* "one", -*ɓili* "two" and -*tatu* "three". These roots are attached to concords, which depend on the class of the noun being counted, and are placed after the noun:

Class	Concord	Example
1	u-	*muntu umozi* "one person"
2	ɓa-	*ɓantu ɓaɓili* "two people"
		ɓantu ɓatatu "three people"
3	u-	*mwala umozi* "one stone"
4	i- / zi-	*miyala ziɓili* "two stones"
		miyala zitatu "three stones"
5	i-	*motoka imozi* "one car"
6	ya-	*mamotoka yaɓili* "two cars"
		mamotoka yatatu "three cars"
7	chi-	*chintu chimozi* "one thing"
8	vi-	*vintu viɓili* "two things"
		vintu vitatu "three things"
9	i-	*njovu imozi* "one elephant"
10	zi-	*njovu ziɓili* "two elephants"
		njovu zitatu "three elephants"
12	ka-	*kanyoni kamozi* "one small bird"
13	tu-	*tunyoni tuɓili* "two small birds"
		tunyoni tutatu "three small birds"
14	u-	*usiku umozi* "one night"

Numbers above three are given in English, using the following construction, which incorporates the concord plus the verb -*li* "is/are" (page 24):

mendo yali four "four legs" (literally "legs they're four")
ng'ombe zili ten "ten cows" (literally "cows they're ten")

"Once", "twice", and so on, are indicated by the prefix *ka-* (*kamozi, kaɓili, katatu*). Again, numbers above three are given in English (*kali four* "four times").

"First", "second", "third", and so on, are most commonly translated as in the examples below, with the numbers in English:

Ni mukazi waɓo wa number three "She's his third wife"
ɓamapumula pa day ya number seven "They rest on the seventh day"

Possession

Possession is indicated using concords which depend on the class of the noun. These concords (underlined) can either join two nouns, like the word "of"...

>nyumba <u>ya</u> imbwa "the dog's house" ("house of the dog")
>chakudya <u>cha</u> imbwa "the dog's food" ("food of the dog")

... or can be put together with the suffixes -nga "mine", -ko "yours" (singular), -ke "his/hers", -tu "ours", -nu "yours" (plural or respectful), -βo "theirs":

>nyumba <u>ya</u>nga "my house"   nyumba <u>ya</u>tu "our house"
>nyumba <u>ya</u>ko "your house" (singular)   nyumba <u>ya</u>nu "your house" (plural)
>nyumba <u>ya</u>ke "his/her house"   nyumba <u>ya</u>βo "their house"

These suffixes can also be attached directly to a few nouns. For example:

>munza<u>ng</u>a "my friend"   munza<u>tu</u> "our friend"
>munza<u>ko</u> "your friend" (singular)   munza<u>nu</u> "your house" (plural)
>munza<u>ke</u> "his/her friend"   munza<u>βo</u> "their friend"

The possessive concords for each class are as follows...

Class	Concord	Example
1	wa-	mwana <u>wa</u>βo "their child"
2	βa-	βana <u>βa</u>βo "their children"
3	wa-	mutu <u>wa</u>ko "your head"
4	ya- / za-	mitu <u>ya</u>nu / mitu <u>za</u>nu "your heads"
5	ya-	motoka <u>ya</u>nga "my car"
6	ya-	mamotoka <u>ya</u>tu "our cars"
7	cha-	chipyango <u>cha</u> mukazi "the woman's broom"
8	va-	vipyango <u>va</u> βakazi "the women's brooms"
9	ya-	mbuzi <u>ya</u>nga "my goat"
10	za-	mbuzi <u>za</u>nga "my goats"
12	ka-	kashimi <u>ka</u> βana "the children's story"
13	twa-	tushimi <u>twa</u> βana "the children's stories"
14	wa-	umoyo <u>wa</u> imbwa "the dog's life"
15	kwa-	kusegula <u>kwa</u> shop "opening of the shop"
16	pa-	pansi <u>pa</u> mwala "under the stone"
17	kwa-	kumbali <u>kwa</u> mumana "beside the river"
18	mwa-	mukati <u>mwa</u> nyumba "inside the house"

When describing the place that a person or thing belongs to, the possessive concord is followed by pa-, ku- or mu- (see page 16):

muntu wa ku Zambia "Zambian person" (literally "person of at Zambia")
nsimbi ya mu motoka "car part" (literally "metal of in car")

Possessive concords can also be used to link a noun to a verb, for example:

mpepo yakupya "hot air" (from *kupya* "to be hot")
ntawi yakudya "meal time" (from *kudya* "to eat")

With longer verbs, *-aku-* is usually shortened to *-o-*:

manamba yosoβa "missing numbers" (from *kusoβa* "to be missing")
βana βodwala "sick children" (from *kudwala* "to be ill")

Nouns describing a type of person may be prefixed with *waku-* or *o-* (a shortening of *wo-*) meaning "one who":

okondwela "happy person" (from *kukondwela* "to be happy")

Similarly, the names of things may begin with *chaku-* or *cho-* "that which":

chakudya "food" ("that which is eaten", from *kudya* "to eat")
chovala "clothing" ("that which is worn", from *kuvala* "to wear")

A longer way of saying "that/which/who" is using *-mene* prefixed by the possessive concord:

kulibe wamene anganipase chikondi chamene umanipasa
"there's nobody who can give me the love that you give me"

In such constructions *-amene* is often shortened to *-e...*

ndiye che (chamene) nikonda "that's what I like"
sinifuna kuziβa ve (vamene) unachita "I don't want to know what you did"

Po- or *pamene* means "at the place which" or "at the time which"...

anakwiya pamene anaβaona "she was angry when she saw them"
poyenda kunyumba "on the way home"

Mo- or *mwamene* means "in the way which" or "how"...

nimakuona mwamene umanisunshila
"I see the way you shake your behind at me"

munionese mogwilila shovel "show me how to hold the shovel"

Location

To express location, a noun is prefixed with either:

- *pa-*, which roughly means "on" and indicates a precise spot
- *ku-*, which roughly means "to" and indicates a more general location
- *mu-*, which means "in" and indicates a location inside something

Words prefixed with *pa-*, *ku-* and *mu-* form distinct noun classes, with their own concords (underlined in the example below):

pa̲ziko pa̲no pa̲li mavuto "in this world there are troubles"
mu̲munzi mu̲ja mu̲li nkuku "in that village there are chickens"

The related suffixes *-po*, *-ko* and *-mo* are commonly found on verbs, and loosely translate as "here" or "there":

word yamene yasoβapo̲ "the word that is missing there"
nifunako̲ tandizo "I want help here"

There are also possessive forms *pa-*, *kwa-* and *mwa-* meaning "of a place" (see page 14). *Kwa-* is used when referring to a place where someone stays rather a place that they own. Compare:

kunyumba kwa̲nga "at my house" (in which I stay)
kunyumba yanga "at my house" (which I own)

kumunzi kwa̲nu "at your village" (in which you live)
kumunzi wanu "at your village" (of which you are the chief)

Kwa- is also used in place of *ku-* when referring to certain poor areas of town:

kwa Kanyama "in Kanyama compound"

To say that something exists or where it is located, *pa-*, *ku-* or *mu-* is used with the verb *-li* "be" (see page 24):

pa page pa̲li mapikicha "on the page there are pictures"
ku̲li njila ziβili "there are two ways"

To say that something does **not** exist, *-li* is replaced with *-libe*:

kuli̲be nyama zaso "there are no such animals"
pali̲be vuto "no problem"

Another way of expressing "there is" or "there are" uses *-po*, *-ko* or *-mo*:

mulilo ulipo "there is a fire" (literally "a fire is there")
motoka yanga silipo "my car is not there"

Demonstratives

There are four sets of words for "this/that/these/those", depending on how far away (physically and conceptually) the object is:

	Demonstratives	Examples
Near	uno, ino, chino, etc	*motoka ino* "this car" (which we're in)
↑	uyu, iyi, ichi, etc	*motoka iyi* "this car" (beside us)
↓	uyo, iyo, icho, etc	*motoka iyo* "that car" (over there)
Far	uja, ija, chija, etc	*motoka ija* "that car" (previously mentioned)

The demonstrative can go either before or after the noun (*motoka iyi* or *iyi motoka*), with a subtle difference in emphasis but the same basic meaning.

All these words vary according to the noun class of the object they refer to. Their forms are derived from the concords on page 13:

Class	Examples	
1/2	<u>uyu</u> muntu "this person"	<u>aβa</u> βantu "these people"
3/4	<u>uyu</u> mugodi "this hole"	<u>izi</u> migodi "these holes"
5/6	<u>iyi</u> banana "this banana"	<u>aya</u> mabanana "these bananas"
7/8	<u>ichi</u> chintu "this thing"	<u>ivi</u> vintu "these things"
9/10	<u>iyi</u> nyama "this animal"	<u>izi</u> nyama "these animals"
12/13	<u>aka</u> kanyoni "this little bird"	<u>utu</u> tunyoni "these little birds"
14	<u>uyu</u> umoyo "this life"	

Words for "here" and "there" are formed in a similar way, using the concords for the locative classes *pa-*, *ku-*, and *mu-* (see page 16):

pano "here" (on the spot where I am)   *apa* "here" (on this spot beside me)
kuno "here" (at the place where I am)   *uku* "here" (at this place beside me)
muno "here" (in the thing I'm in)   *umu* "here" (in this thing beside me)

apo "there" (on that spot over there)   *paja* "there" (on the spot mentioned)
uko "there" (in that area over there)   *kuja* "there" (at the place mentioned)
umo "there" (in that thing over there)   *muja* "there" (in the thing mentioned)

When identifying a thing or a place, the following construction is common:

Ni chamene ichi "It's this one here" (literally "It's that which is this")
Ni pamene apa "It's this place here"

Verbs

Nearly all verbs in Nyanja end with -*a* (which changes to -*e* in certain situations). Verbs in a real-life sentence nearly always have prefixes attached. When unprefixed verb roots are cited in books, they are generally preceded with a dash:

    -*menya* "hit"   -*vina* "dance"

Verbs derived from English also end in -*a* when borrowed into Nyanja:

    -*washa* "wash"   -*chinja* "change"

Sometimes the English ending -*ing* is also incorporated:

    -*flashing'a* "flush"   -*cheking'a* "check"

English verbs that don't fit this structure can usually only be included in a Nyanja sentence if they are preceded by the verb -*chita* "do":

    Tachita repair motoka "We repaired the car" ("did a repair")
    Niyenda kuchita print ma papers "I'm going to print the papers"

In their infinitive forms, or when used as nouns, verbs are prefixed with *ku-* "to":

    kumenya "to hit" / "hitting"   *kuvina* "to dance" / "dancing"

Other prefixes and suffixes attached to a verb provide information about when, how and with whom an action takes place. A phrase containing a verb such as -*ona* "see" may include (in this order) the following components:

Negation	**Subject**	**Tense**
Niona "I see"	*Niona* "I see"	*Niona* "I see"
Siniona "I don't see"	*Aona* "He sees"	*Ninaona* "I saw"
	Tiona "We see"	*Nizaona* "I will see"

Object	**Extensions**	**Mood**
Niona "I see"	*Niona* "I see"	*Niona* "I see"
Nikuona "I see you"	*Nioneka* "I'm seen"	*Nione* "Let me see"
Niziona "I see myself"	*Nionesa* "I make seen"	

These are explained in more detail on the following pages.

In most cases such phrases are pronounced with a high tone on the tense marker (*Nináona* "I saw", *Tizáona* "We'll see"). A notable exception is the tense used for completed actions or states, in which the tense marker and the subject pronoun combine into a single syllable and the high tone is on the first syllable of the verb instead (*Aóna* "He has seen", which contrasts with **Á**ona "He sees").

Subject and object

The following prefixes indicate the subject of a verb:

Prefix	Subject	Example
ni-	"I"	ni̱funa "I want"
u-	"you" (singular)	u̱funa "you want"
a-	"he/she"	a̱funa "he/she wants"
i- & variants	"it"	i̱funa "it wants"
ti-	"we"	ti̱funa "we want"
mu-	"you" (plural/respectful)	mu̱funa "you want"
βa-& variants	"they"	βa̱funa "they want"

The following particles are placed after the subject and any tense marker to indicate the object of an action:

Prefix	Object	Example
-ni-	"me"	βani̱funa "they want me"
-ku-	"you" (singular)	βaku̱funa "they want you"
-mu-	"him/her"	βamu̱funa "they want him/her"
-i- & variants	"it"	βaifuna "they want it"
-ti-	"us"	βati̱funa "they want us"
-ku-...-ni	"you" (plural/respectful)	βaku̱funani̱ "they want you"
-βa- & variants	"them"	βaβa̱funa "they want them"

When the subject or object is inanimate, "it/they/them" may be *i-, u-, chi-, vi-, zi-, ka-,* or *tu-,* depending on the class of the noun. These prefixes are the same as the concords listed on page 13. In the examples in this chapter, "it" is translated as *i-,* which is the most common form, and "them" is translated as *βa-,* which is the form used for people.

Reflexive actions (performed on oneself) are indicated with a marker *-zi-:*

nizimenya "I hit myself" tizimenya "we hit ourselves"
uzimenya "you hit yourself" muzimenya "you hit yourselves"
azimenya "he/she hits him/herself" βazimenya "they hit themselves"
izimenya "it hits itself"

Note, however, that the interpretation of the marker *-zi-* depends on the tone:

nízimvela "I listen to myself" (high tone on first syllable)
nizímvela "I should listen" (high tone on second syllable)

Negation

"Not" is usually indicated by *si-*, which combines with the subject prefixes (for example, *si-* & *u-* combine to make *su-*) as in the examples below:

<u>si</u>niyenda "I don't go" <u>si</u>tiyenda "we don't go"
<u>su</u>yenda "you don't go" <u>si</u>muyenda "you don't go"
<u>sa</u>yenda "he/she doesn't go" <u>si</u>βayenda "they don't go"
<u>si</u>yenda "it doesn't go"

With negative forms in the past tense, the final -a of the verb changes to -e:

si<u>ni</u>nayend<u>e</u> "I didn't go"

In certain forms, such as when giving prohibitions (page 28), the negative marker becomes -*sa-*:

Ananiuza ati ni<u>sa</u>yende "He told me not to go"
O<u>sa</u>yenda! "Don't go!"

Tense and mood

Tense and mood are mostly indicated using short markers (underlined in the examples below) that are placed after the subject prefix. In addition, the final -a of a verb changes to -e in some forms:

ni<u>ta</u>ndiza "I'm helping" *ni<u>za</u>tandiza* "I will help"
n<u>a</u>tandiza "I've helped" *ni<u>zaka</u>tandiza* "I might help"
ni<u>ma</u>tandiza "I help" (habitually) *ni<u>nga</u>tandiz<u>e</u>* "I can help"
ni<u>na</u>tandiza "I helped" *ni<u>ka</u>tandiz<u>e</u>* "I should help"

The ordinary **present tense** is not usually marked in any particular way. However, with short verbs where the verb root comprises just one syllable, the present tense is marked with *-ku-*:

ni<u>ku</u>dya "I'm eating"
βa<u>ku</u>mwa "they're drinking"

An action which has just been completed, or a **state** which persists up to the present, is indicated by adding *-a-*. This combines with the subject prefixes (for example, *ni-* & *-a-* combine to make *na-*) as in the examples below:

n<u>a</u>dwala "I'm ill" t<u>a</u>dwala "we're ill"
w<u>a</u>dwala "you're ill" mw<u>a</u>dwala "you're ill"
<u>a</u>dwala "he/she's ill" β<u>a</u>dwala "they're ill"
y<u>a</u>dwala "it's ill"

Descriptive verbs such as -nana "be wet" are most commonly in this form, though they may be in the present tense instead if a state has not been fully achieved:

shati yanana "the shirt has got wet / the shirt is wet" (a state)
shati inana "the shirt is getting wet" (present tense)

In certain contexts this form can also be used for an action that hasn't yet occurred but will be completed very shortly (e.g. *Nabwela* "I'm about to come").

The **simple past tense** is marked with -na-:

ni<u>na</u>mvela "I heard" ti<u>na</u>mvela "we heard"
u<u>na</u>mvela "you heard" mu<u>na</u>mvela "you heard"
a<u>na</u>mvela "he/she heard" β<u>ana</u>mvela "they heard"
i<u>na</u>mvela "it heard"

In Town Nyanja the **continuous past tense** is indicated by forms based on -enze followed by the *ku-* form of the verb. This combines with the subject prefixes as shown in the examples below:

n<u>enze</u> kuyenda "I was going" t<u>enze</u> kuyenda "we were going"
w<u>enze</u> kuyenda "you were going" mw<u>enze</u> kuyenda "you were going"
<u>enze</u> kuyenda "he/she was going" β<u>enze</u> kuyenda "they were going"
y<u>enze</u> kuyenda "it was going"

-*enze* + *ku-* can be shortened to -*enzo-* (e.g. *nenzoyenda* "I was going").

The -*enze* forms can also be put together with **other past tense forms** to indicate that an action has already been completed (e.g. *nenze nayenda* "I'd gone") or that it occurred in the distant past (e.g. *nenze ninayenda* "I went").

In negative forms, *si-* "not" combines with *enze* to form *senze* (e.g. <u>senze</u> *kuyenda* "he wasn't going").

Activities which are carried out **habitually** are marked with -ma-:

ni<u>ma</u>yimba ku church "I sing at church"
ti<u>ma</u>kumana pa Thursday "we meet on Thursdays"

Repeated or chaotic actions can be indicated by doubling (reduplicating) the verb:

Malaiti yama<u>yenda</u>-yenda "The electricity keeps coming and going"

The simple **future tense** is indicated by -za-:

ni<u>za</u>bwela "I will come" ti<u>za</u>bwela "we will come"
u<u>za</u>bwela "you will come" mu<u>za</u>bwela "you will come"
a<u>za</u>bwela "he/she will come" β<u>aza</u>bwela "they will come"
i<u>za</u>bwela "it will come"

A more uncertain future is marked by *-zaka-* (e.g. *niza̱kabwela* "I might come").

Ability to do something is indicated by *-nga-* "can", with the final *-a* of the verb changing to *-e*:

Anga̱imilile̱ mukati "He can stand up inside"
Sininga̱tamange̱ "I can't run"

Future **possibilities** or **conditions** ("when" or "if") can be indicated with *-ka-* (see also page 30):

Nika̱mwa moβa nimabema fwaka "When I drink beer I smoke tobacco"
Nimabema fwaka nika̱mwa moβa "I smoke tobacco when I drink"

Hypothetical actions which didn't actually happen ("would have" or "should have") are preceded with the word *sembe*:

Sembe nenze nayenda "I should have gone"
Sembe sinayenda "I shouldn't have gone"

Sembe bus sinaimilile, sembe afa
 "If the bus hadn't stopped, he would have died"

Verb extensions

There are various endings which can be added to a verb to alter its meaning...

For **reciprocal** actions (things done to one another), the verb ends in *-ana*:

-ona "see" *-onana* "see each other"
-menya "hit" *-menyana* "fight" ("hit each other")

The **stative** ending *-eka* or *-ika* means "be in a state of being...":

-ona "see" *-oneka* "be visible" ("be seen")
-funa "want / need" *-funika* "be needed"

(*-ika* is used when the verb root contains *a*, *i* or *u*, as in *fu̱nika*, and *-eka* is used elsewhere. A similar pattern applies to the other extensions described below.)

The **applicative** ending *-ela* or *-ila* generally occurs when a verb is applied to an indirect object:

-choka "come out" *-chokela* "come out of / come from"
-jumpa "jump" *-jumpila* "jump into / jump onto"

However, sometimes it alters the meaning of a verb in unpredictable ways:

-kondewa "be loved" *-kondwela* "be happy"
-nunka "smell bad" *-nunkila* "smell good"

Constructions with the applicative ending are often used where English speakers would use prepositions such as "for" and "to":

Nizakumenya "I'll beat you"
Nizakumenyela "I'll fight for you"

The double ending *-elela* or *-ilila* indicates that an action happens in a fixed place:

-ima "get up / stand up"   *-imilila* "stand still"
-gwila "grab / hold"   *-gwililila* "hold in place"

Some Nyanja verbs have a form ending in *-ka* describing one's own state, and a form ending in *-la* describing an action carried out on another object:

-nyamuka "stand up" (oneself)   *-nyamula* "lift / carry" (something)
-beuka "flip over" (oneself)   *-beula* "flip over" (something)

There are various **causative** endings meaning "to make something happen". The most common is *-esa* or *-isa*:

-ziβa "know"   *-ziβisa* "introduce" (make something known)
-gwa "fall"   *-gwesa* "drop" (make something fall)

With descriptive verbs, these endings can signify "very" or "too much":

-kula "become big"   *-kulisa* "be too big"
-chepa "become small"   *-chepesa* "be too small"

Some other causative endings are illustrated below:

-yenda "go"   *-yenza* "drive" (make something go)
-fendela "move" (oneself)   *-fendeza* "move" (make something move)

-ima "get up"   *-imya* "lift up"
-zima "be extinguished"   *-zimya* "extinguish"

-uka "wake up" (oneself)   *-usha* "wake up" (make someone wake)
-yaka "be alight"   *-yasha* "light up" (make something alight)

There is an ending *-ewa* or *-iwa* which makes a verb **passive**:

-itana "call"   *-itaniwa* "be called"
-panga "make"   *-pangiwa* "be made"

However, Nyanja speakers generally prefer active sentences ("They did it") to passive ones ("It was done").

To be and to have

In the present and past tense, the verb "be" is -li:

Nili... "I am..."   *Nenzeli...* "I was..."
Uli... "You are..."   *Wenzeli...* "You were..." (singular)
Ali... "He/she is..."   *Enzeli...* "He/she was..."
Ili... "It is..."   *Yenzeli...* "It was..."
Tili... "We are..."   *Tenzeli...* "We were..."
Muli... "You are..."   *Mwenzeli...* "You were..." (plural)
βali... "They are..."   *βenzeli...* "They were..."

This is used when describing or locating something:

Muli kuti? "Where are you?"
Pamene nenzeli bebi... "When I was a baby..."

In standard Nyanja, *-li* is also widely used in combination with other verbs to make compound tenses (like in English "He is doing"). Such forms have largely fallen out of use in Town Nyanja, but the following construction is still used:

Nika<u>li</u> kumwa moβa "I <u>am</u> still drinking beer"

In the future tense, *-li* is never used. Instead, "be" is translated using the verb *-nkala* "sit":

Tiza<u>nkala</u> βantanzi "We will be healthy"
Ningakondwele ku<u>nkala</u> munzako "I would like to be your friend"

"It is" or "they are" can also be translated using the word *ni*. This is used when identifying an object or its owner:

Iyi <u>ni</u> yanga "This is mine"
<u>Ni</u> βana βamene βamavidya "It's the children who eat them"

To say who a person is, there are special forms *ndine* "I am", *ndiwe* or *ndimwe* "you are", *ndise* "we are", and *ndiye* "he/she is" or "they are":

Iwe <u>ndiwe</u> munzanga "You are my friend"
Si<u>ndine</u> chipyango "I am not a broom" (line from a song)

In Nyanja there is no verb "have" to indicate who possesses something. Instead, speakers say *-li na* or *-nkala na* "be with":

Ali <u>na</u> matu yakulu "He has big ears" ("He is with big ears")
Tifunika ku<u>nkala</u> <u>na</u> manzi "We need to have water" ("...be with water")

Pronouns

Personal pronouns most commonly take the form of prefixes attached to a verb (see page 19). These are underlined in the examples below:

> ni̱naβaona "I̱ saw them"   βana̱niona "They saw me̱"
> ti̱naβaona "We̱ saw them"   βana̱tiona "They saw us̱"

However, there is also a set of separate pronouns:

> ine "me"   ise "us"
> iwe "you" (singular)   imwe "you" (plural / respectful)
> eve "him/her"   βeve "them"

These pronouns can be used on their own – as in the use of *Iwe!* "You!" to get someone's attention – or can be included in a sentence for emphasis:

> *Ine* nakonzeka "Me, I'm ready"
> Osayope *iwe* "You, don't be afraid"

"By oneself" is expressed using derivatives of these pronouns which end in *-eka*:

> neka "by myself"   teka "by ourselves"
> weka "by yourself"   mweka "by yourselves"
> eka "by himself/herself"   βeka "by themselves"

"All" or "every" is expressed using forms ending in *-onse*:

> tonse "all of us"
> monse "all of you"
> βonse "all of them"

There are also forms ending with *-ina* meaning "one" or "some" or "any", and forms ending with *-inangu* meaning "another" or "others" (some speakers don't distinguish between the *-ina* and *-inangu* forms):

> wina "one of you"   βena "some of them"
> winangu "another of you"   βenangu "others of them"

Na- "and/with" can combine with certain pronouns in special contracted forms:

> Tiyeni *naye* muntu uyu "Let's go with him, this person"
> vovala vamene uyenda *navo* "the clothes with which you're going"

However, in other cases there is no contraction:

> Ine *naβeve* tichokela ku London "Me and them, we come from London"
> *Naiwe*, ungabwele "You too, you can come"

With inanimate objects, such pronouns have different forms depending on the noun class (see page 10) of the object being referred to:

Class	Examples	
3/4	*munda onse* "all of the field" *munda winangu* "another field" *weve* "it" *nao* "with it"	*minda zonse* "all of the fields" *minda zinangu* "other fields" *yeve / zeve* "them" *nayo / nazo* "with them"
5/6	*tupi yonse* "all of the body" *tupi inangu* "another body" *yeve* "it" *nayo* "with it"	*matupi yonse* "all of the bodies" *matupi yenangu* "other bodies" *yeve* "them" *nayo* "with them"
7/8	*[chintu] chonse* "all of the thing" *[chintu] chinangu* "another thing" *cheve* "it" *nacho* "with it"	*[vintu] vonse* "all of the things" *[vintu] vinangu* "other things" *veve* "them" *navo* "with them"
9/10	*mbuzi yonse* "all of the goat" *mbuzi inangu* "another goat" *yeve* "it" *nayo* "with it"	*mbuzi zonse* "all of the goats" *mbuzi zinangu* "other goats" *zeve* "them" *nazo* "with them"
12/13	*kashimi konse* "all of the story" *kashimi kenangu* "another story" *keve* "it" *nako* "with it"	*tushimi tonse* "all of the stories" *tushimi twinangu* "other stories" *tweve* "them" *nato* "with them"
14	*moβa onse* "all of the beer" *moβa winangu* "another beer" *weve* "it" *nao* "with it"	

There are also pronouns referring to locations, based on the prefixes *pa-*, *ku-* and *mu-* (see page 16):

ponse "everywhere"
penangu "somewhere else"
peve "there" (on a particular spot)

monse "everywhere"
mwinangu "somewhere else"
mweve "there" (inside something)

konse "everywhere"
kwinangu "somewhere else"
kweve "there" (in a general area)

Describing things

Nyanja has only a few true adjectives. These come after the noun they describe, and are prefixed with the concords shown on page 13 (except in the case of class 1 nouns, denoting humans, with which the prefix on the adjective is *mu-* not *u-*):

-kulu "big, wide"	**Example:** *imbwa ikulu* "big dog"
-ng'ono "small, narrow"	*kamwana kang'ono* "small child"
-tali "long, tall, far"	*muntu mutali* "tall person"
-fupi "short, near"	*ruler ifupi* "short ruler"

Many of the other concepts which we describe using adjectives in English are described using verbs in Nyanja. For example, instead of an adjective "tired" there is a verb *-lema* "be tired". As the examples below show, this behaves grammatically in the same way as an ordinary verb such as *-fika* "arrive"...

Nafika "I've arrived" *Nalema* "I'm tired"
Wafika? "Have you arrived?" *Walema?* "Are you tired?"
βazafika "They'll arrive" *βazalema* "They'll be tired"

A noun can also be described using another noun, linked using a possessive concord (page 14). For example:

mwana wa ulesi "lazy child" ("child of laziness")
answer ya zoona "correct answer" ("answer of truth")

This construction is also used for adjectives borrowed from English:

manzi ya clean "clean water"
chakudya cha fresh "fresh food"

Comparisons can be made using *pali* "be on top of" or *kuchila* "to surpass":

nyumba yanga ni ikulu <u>pali</u> yako "my house is bigger than yours"
or *nyumba yanga ni ikulu <u>kuchila</u> yako*

There is no specific way to express superlatives such as "biggest". These are generally translated using expressions such as:

nyumba yanga ndiye ikulu maningi mumunzi
"my house is the very big one in the village"

To make it absolutely clear that the thing being referred to is the greatest, it is necessary to say something like:

nyumba yanga ni ikulu kuchila manyumba yenangu yali mumunzi
"my house is big, surpassing the other houses that are in the village"

Instructions

A simple, informal instruction can consist of a verb on its own. However, when giving instructions to more than one person or showing respect the verb is suffixed with -ni.

Ima! "Get up!" (singular)   *Imani* "Please get up" (plural / respectful)
Bwela! "Come!"   *Bwelani* "Please come"

Instructions that would otherwise consist of only one syllable are prefixed with *i-*:

Idya! "Eat!"   *Dyani* "Please eat"
Imwa! "Drink!"   *Mwani* "Please drink"

In less direct requests or suggestions, and whenever a subject or object prefix is attached, the final *-a* of the verb changes to *-e*:

Tiyende (or *Tiye*) "Let's go"
Niitenge "Let me take it"
Nifuna muimilile "I want you to stand"
Anaβauza kuti βabwele "He asked them to come"

Politeness may be achieved by putting the verb in an indirect form, using the applicative ending described on page 22:

Nipase manzi "Give me water" (direct and impolite)
Nipasileko manzi "Pass the water here for me" (less direct)

When the verb is suffixed with *-ko*, *-po* or *-mo* (page 16), as in the example above, the plural/respectful suffix *-ni* is repeated:

Nipasilenikoni manzi "Please pass the water there to me"

Instructions may be prefixed with *ka-* meaning "go and...". Again the verb ends with *-e*:

Kasambe "Go and bathe"

Actions that "should be" done are marked by *-zi-*:

Uzinimvelela "You should be listening to me"
Muzipempela "You should be praying"

In prohibitions (when asking someone not to do something), the verb is prefixed with *osa-* (singular) or *mosa-* (plural or respectful):

Osanimenya "Don't hit me!"
Mosachita ichi "Please don't do this"

Questions

Questions are typically phrased the same way as statements, but said with a different tone of voice:

Alikò "He's here" (voice falls on the last syllable)
Alikó? "Is he here?" (voice rises on the last syllable)

Questions are sometimes begun with *nanga*, particularly when they follow on from something else that has been said:

<u>Nanga</u> ufuna chani? "So what do you want?"

Alternatively, questions may end with *ka?* (this also occurs in Zambian English):

Tiyenda, <u>ka</u>? "We're going, aren't we?"

The Bemba question marker *Bushe* may also be heard from speakers of Town Nyanja. *Bushe mushe?* ("Good?") is a common greeting. The standard Nyanja question marker *kodi* is not used much in Town Nyanja.

To ask "which?", use *-ti* prefixed with one of the concords on page 13, according to the noun class of the thing being referred to:

Ni <u>iti</u> motoka yanu? "Which is your car?"
Ni <u>viti</u> vintu vanu? "Which are your things?"

Put together with the locative prefix *pa-*, *ku-* or *mu-* (page 16), this forms *pati?*, *kuti?* or *muti?* "where?". As always, the *pa-* form implies a specific spot, the *ku-* form a general location, and the *mu-* form an interior location.

"How much?" or "how many?" is *-ngati*, again with a prefix depending on the noun class. When asking about prices it is *zingati?*, concording with the noun class of *ndalama* "money". When counting people it is *Bangati?*.

Other question words include:

Chani? "What?"

Ndani? "Who?" (plural or respectful form: *Bandani?*)

Liti? "When?" (or *Ntawi bwanji?* "What time?")

Bwanji? "How?" (this can also mean "Which one?" in certain contexts)

It is common to hear shortenings of question words, such as *cha?* for *chani?*, *nda?* for *ndani?*, *bwa?* for *bwanjii?* and *zinga?* for *zingati?*.

Conjunctions

Many of the conjunctions used in Town Nyanja are borrowed from other languages such as English:

    na "and"   *then* "[and] then"
    olo "or"   *so* "so"
    bati / koma "but"   *chifukwa / ndaβa* "because"

A series of actions can be joined with *naku-* (sometimes shortened to *no-*):

    βabwela <u>naku</u>bisama "They come and hide"
    Anajumpa <u>naku</u>tamangila panja "He jumped up and ran outside"

"When" or "if" is translated using the word *ngati*, placed either at the start of the sentence or in between two phrases, with a slight difference in meaning:

    <u>Ngati</u> namwa moβa nimabema fwaka "When I drink beer I smoke tobacco"
    Nimabema fwaka <u>ngati</u> namwa moβa "If I drink beer then I smoke tobacco"

"When" or "if" can also be indicated using the verb marker *-ka-* (see page 22).

An additional clause in a sentence may be introduced with *kuti* "that":

    Osayende lelo <u>kuti</u> mukayendele pamozi
    "Don't go today [so that] you can go together"

When reporting speech, *ati* is normally used instead of *kuti*:

    Akamba <u>ati</u> ayenda ku church "He said he's going to church"
    (In speech the vowels are commonly run together to make *Akambati...*)

Ati is used whenever a speaker is introducing second-hand information; it indicates that something is not the speaker's own words:

    <u>Ati</u> βantu βayopa "I hear that people are scared"

There are related forms such as *nati* "I said..." and *wati* or *mwati* "you said...".

    <u>Wati</u> cha? "What did you say?"
    <u>Nati</u> nizabwela "I said I'll come"

However, the use of such forms in Town Nyanja is much more limited than in standard Nyanja (in which *-ti* is a general verb meaning "say").

Useful phrases

Basics

Hi	Bwanji	*I think...*	Niganiza...
How are you?	Muli bwanji?	*What's this?*	Nichichani ichi?
I'm fine	Nili bwino / Nili mushe	*I don't know*	Siniziβa
And you?	Nanga imwe?	*Do you speak English?*	Muziβa kukamba Chizungu?
Good morning	Mwauka bwanji? ("How did you wake?")	*I don't speak Nyanja*	Siniziβa kukamba Chinyanja / Sinimakamba Chinyanja
Response:	Nauka bwino		
Good afternoon	Mwachoma bwanji?	*I speak a bit of Nyanja*	Nimakamba pang'ono Chinyanja
Response:	Nachoma bwino		
Good night	Mugone bwino ("Sleep well")	*I'm learning to speak Nyanja*	Nipunzila kukamba Chinyanja
Goodbye	Muyende bwino ("Go well") Musale bwino ("Remain well")	*I don't understand*	Sinimvela
		I didn't hear [what you said]	Sininamvele [vamene mwakamba]
See you	Tizaonana		
Excuse me	Zikomo	*Please repeat that*	Bwezani poni nafuti
Sorry	Sorry		
Yes	E-e	*Please speak slowly*	Kambani pang'ono-pang'ono
No	Iyayi		
Thank you [very much]	Zikomo [kwambili]	*How do you say ... in Nyanja?*	Mumakamba bwanji ... mu Chinyanja?
I want...	Nifuna...	*Did I say it right?*	Nanga naikamba bwino?
I don't want...	Sinifuna...		
I like...	Nikonda...		
I don't like	Sinikonda...		

Describing people

English	Chinyanja
What's your name?	Zina yako ndiwe ndani? *(informal)* / Zina yanu ndimwe βandani? *(respectful)*
My name is...	Zina yanga ndine...
How old are you? *(to a child or a friend)*	Uli na ma *years* yangati? / Uli na zingati *years*?
I am ... years old	Nili na ... *years*
Are you married?	Ndimwe βokwatiliwa?
How many children do you have?	Muli na βana βangati?
I have...	Nili na...
one child	mwana umozi
two children	βana βaβili
three children	βana βatatu
four children	βana βali *four*
I don't have any children	Nilibe βana
This is...	Uyu ni...
my husband	mwamuna wanga
my wife	mukazi wanga
my child	mwana wanga
my older brother/sister	mukulu wanga
my younger brother/sister	mufana wanga
my father	βatate βanga
my mother	βamai βanga
my friend	munzanga
I'm on holiday	Nili pa *holiday*
I live here	Ninkala kuno
Where are you from?	[Nanga imwe] munkala kuti?
I'm from...	Nichokela ku...
I live at...	Ninkala ku...
I live in...	Ninkala mu...
What tribe do you belong to?	Ndimwe βatundu bwanji?
Did you grow up here?	Munakulila muno *(in an area)* / Munakulila kuno *(at a place)*
I was born in...	Ninabadwila ku...
My parents come from...	Makolo βanga βachokela ku...
How many years have you been in Zambia?	Mwankala ma *years* yangati mu Zambia?
I like it here	Nakondako kuno
The weather is nice	*Weather* ni yabwino
The people are friendly	βantu ni βabwino mitima

Getting around

Where are you going?	Muyenda kuti?
I'm going to...	Niyenda ku...
We're going to...	Tiyenda ku...
Is it open?	Nanga ni yosegula?
What time do they open?	βamasegula ntawi bwanji?
What time do they close?	βavala ntawi bwanji?
It's open from ... to ...	Ni kosegula kuchoka ... kufika ...
Is there an entrance fee?	βalipilisa pongena?
What time will we leave?	Tizanyamuka ntawi bwanji?
What time will we get back?	Tizabwelako ntawi bwanji?
Is this the way to... ?	Ndiye njila yamene iyenda ku... ?
How can I get to... ?	Ningayende bwanji ku... ?
How can I get there?	Nizayendako bwanji kuja?
I want to travel by car	Nifuna kuyenda na motoka
Will my car cope with the road?	Nanga motoka yanga ingakwanise kupita mu road?
I want to walk	Nifuna kuyenda na mendo
It's too far to walk	Ni patali ngati muyenda na mendo
Should I take a taxi?	Ningayende na taxi?
Where is/are...	Ni kuti ku...

Names of places such as "post office", "bank", "restaurant" etc are usually the same as in English.

It's near here	Ni pafupi na kuno
It's far from here	Ni patali na kuno
Give me directions	Nilangizeni moyendela
To the left	Ku *left*
To the right	Ku *right*
Go straight on	Yendani pasogolo
Cross the road	Jumpani njila
Go past the...	Mupitilile pa...
It's the first gate	Ni *gate* yoyamba (*gate* ya namba 1)
It's the second gate	Ni *gate* ya namba 2
It's near the...	Ni pafupi na...
It's 10 minutes by car	Ni ma *minute* 10 ngati muyenda na motoka
It's 10 minutes on foot	Ni ma *minute* 10 ngati muyenda na mendo

Where's the nearest bus stop?	Bus stop yapafupi ili kuti?	The tyre's flat	Tyre yapompoloka / Tyre yaponcha
Where's the bus for... ?	Bus yaku ... ili kuti?	Please fill up the car	Nifakilenikoni *fuel* mu motoka
Which is the bus for...	Ni iti *bus* yaku...	Please pump up my tyre	Nipompelenikoni *tyre*
Is this the right bus for... ?	Iyi ndiye *bus* yamene iyenda ku...	The car's broken down	Motoka yafa (literally "it's dead")
Where is the driver?	βa *driver* βali kuti?	Is there a garage nearby?	Pali *garage* pafupi?
How much is the fare?	Ni zingati kulipila? / Mulipilisa zingati?	Can you fix it?	Mungakwanise kuikonza? / Munganikonzeleko?
Can I have my change?	Munganipase *change* yanga?	We need to replace...	Tifunika kuchinja...
Where can I drop off?	Ningaselukile pati/kuti?	When will it be fixed?	Izakonzewa liti? / Izalunga liti?
Stop here	Imililani pano/apa	Can you do it now?	Mungakwanise kuchita manje?
How many hours does it take to get to...	Ni mahawa yangati kuti tifike ku...	Park here	Paking'ani apa
Can I go today?	Ningayende lelo?	Please move your car so I can pass	Chosanikoni motoka yanu kuti nipiteko
I want to hire a car	Nifuna kubweleka motoka	Watch where you're going!	Mukaziyangana kwamene muyenda!
Fill it up	Zulikizani		

Accommodation

Do you have a room?	Ma *room* yaliko?
I want a room...	Nifunako *room*...
...for one person	...yogonamo muntu umozi
...for two people	...yogonamo βantu βaβili
I will be staying...	Nizankala...
one day	siku imozi
two days	masiku yaβili
one week	*week* imozi
How much is the room?	Room ni zingati?
I've made a reservation	Nasungiza malo
Please show me the room	Tiyeni munilangize *room*
Is there a bigger one?	Kuliko ikuluko?
Is there anywhere quieter?	Kuli kwamene kuliko zii?
Is there air conditioning?	Muli *air condition*?
Is there hot water?	Kuli manzi yakupya?
Is there another hotel?	Kuliko hotel inangu?
Is breakfast included?	*Breakfast* ilimo?
What time is breakfast?	*Breakfast* ibwela ntawi bwanji?
I'll take this one	Nizatenga [yamene] iyi
You're in room number...	Muli mu *room* ya namba...
Please wake me up at...	Muniushe na....
Please help with my bags	Nitandizeni kunyamula mabagi
It's heavy	Ni cholema
Please send someone to clean the room	Tumanikoni muntu wamene azakilinako room
Is there somewhere I can wash my clothes?	Kuliko kwamene ningawashile vovala vanga?
Is there someone who can wash my clothes?	Kuliko wamene anganiwashileko vovala vanga?
I want to check out	Nifuna kuchoka mu hotel
Please call me a taxi	Niitanilenikoni *taxi*
Please find me a taxi	Nisakililenikoni *taxi*

Shopping

Some of these phrases differ depending on the noun class of the item that is being referred to (page 10). The phrases below are appropriate for artefacts and household objects (class 7/8). For items that are normally associated with class 5/6, such as clothes, replace *chi* or *vi* with *i* or *ya*.

English	Chichewa	English	Chichewa
Give me this/these	Nipaseni ichi/ivi	I'll come back later	Nizabwela nafuti
Where does it come from?	Chichokela kuti?	You're cheating me	Uninama boza
It's nice	Ni chabwino	I'm just looking	Niyangana-yangana chabe
I like it	Nachikonda		
I don't like it	Sininachikonde	I don't have much money	Nilibe ndalama zambili
It's too big	Ni chikulu	Here's the money	Iyi ndalama / Ndalama iyi
It's too small	Ni kang'ono		
It's too expensive	Chadulisa maningi	Where can I buy...?	Ni kuti kwamene ningagule...?
Have you got a cheaper one?	Muli na chochipako?	Do you sell...?	Mumagulisa...
I'll buy it	Nizachigula	Do you accept credit cards?	Mumavomeleza kulipila na *credit card*?
How many?	Ni vingati?		
It doesn't work	Sichiseβenza	If it takes long, I'll just pay by cash	Ngati izachedwa, lekani, nilipile *cash*
Can you give me another?	Munganipase chinangu		
Do you have my size?	Muli na *size* yanga?	Is there an ATM nearby?	Kuliko *ATM* pafupi?
Do you have the colour...?	Muli na *colour* ya...? (colour names are the same as in English)	Where can I change money?	Ni kuti kwamene ningachinjile ndalama?
Can I try it on?	Ningayesemo?	Have you got change for...	Muli na *change* ya...
How much is it?	Ni zingati?	Please give me a receipt	Nipaseni *receipt*
Can you lower the price?	Bwezanikoni mutengo	Please give my money back	Nibwezeleni ndalama zanga

Dining

I want a table for...	Nifuna *table* ya...
two people	βantu βaβili
three people	βantu βatatu
four people	βantu βali *four*
I've saved you a place	Nakusungilani malo
Can we sit in the sunshine?	Tingankale pa zuβa?
Can we sit in the shade?	Tingankale mu chimfwile?
Can we sit by the window?	Tingankale kufupi na *window*
Can I see the menu?	Ningawone *menu*?
What drinks do you have?	Ni vakumwa vabwanji vamene muli navo?
What do you recommend?	Nanga imwe mungasanke iti?
Where can I wash my hands?	Nikuti kwamene ningasambile ku manja?
I don't eat meat	Sinimadya nyama
How long will it be before the food is ready?	Izatenga ntawi bwanji kuti vipye vakudya?
Your food is ready	Vakudya vanu vapya
This isn't what I ordered	Sindiye vamene nagula ivi
The food is hot	Vakudya nivakupya
The food is cold	Vakudya nivozizila
One more, please	Nipasenikoni inangu nafuti
Can I have some salt?	Nipasilenikoni *salt*
Please don't put salt in mine	Osafakamo *salt* mu vakudya vanga
This is delicious	Vamveka bwino/mushe
I don't want anything else	Sinifuna chili chonse
Can I have the bill?	Nipaseni bill
Food	Chakudya / Vakudya
Coffee	Coffee
Tea	Tea
Beer	Moβa
Water	Manzi
Beef	Nyama ya ng'ombe
Pork	Nyama ya nkumba
Chicken	Nkuku
Fish	Nsomba
Nshima	Nsima
Rice	Rice
Beans	Binzi
Maize	Milisi
Sweet potato	Kandolo
Cassava	Kalundwe

Work and business

Where do you work?	Museβenza kuti?
I work here	Niseβenza pano
I work as...	Nigwila nchito ya...
I'm looking for Mr/Mrs...	Nifuna βa Mr/Mrs...
I tried to call but I couldn't get through	Ninayesa kutuma foni, koma sinafike
They're not answering their phone	Siβayanka foni yaβo
When will they be back?	βazabwela liti?
When can we meet?	Tizakumana liti?
Today	Lelo
Tomorrow / yesterday (depending on context)	Mailo
Morning	Kuseni
Afternoon	Muzuβa
Evening	Mumazulo
Now	Manje
At 4 p.m. (exactly)	Pa 16 *hours*
Around 4 p.m.	Ku ma 16 *hours*
What time is it?	Ni ntawi bwanji?
Come in	Ngenani
Come here	Bwelani kuno
Sit down	Nkalani pansi
Wait here	Yembekezani apa/pano
I'm in a hurry	Nili mu *hurry* / Nili *fast*
Who should I speak to?	Ningakambe na βandani?
I want to speak to the manager	Nifuna kukamba na βa *manager*
You've done a good job	Mwagwila nchito yabwino
What you've done is not acceptable	Vamene mwachita sivivomelezewa
Do you understand [what I'm saying]?	Nanga mumvela [vamene nikamba]?
Just tell me the truth	Niuze che vazoona
I think there's been a misunderstanding	Kuoneka simunamvesese
Please put that in writing	Vilembani vamene mwakamba
Help me	Nitandizenikoni
Thank you for your help	Zikomo pakunitandiza

Social / household

Nice to meet you	Zikomo kukumana	Be quiet	Nkalani zii / Osapanga chongo ("Don't make noise")
May I sit here?	Ningankale apa?	Be careful	Muchenjele
Someone is sitting here	Pali βantu pa mupando uyu	Is this dog friendly?	Iyi imbwa siluma?
Can I buy you a drink?	Ningakugulilenikoni *drink*?	I'm hot	Nimvela kupya
Can I smoke?	Ningapepeko fwaka?	I'm cold	Nimvela mpepo
Can I have your number?	Nipempako *phone number* yanu	I'm tired	Nalema
		I'm hungry	Nimvela njala
Beep me so I can get your number too	Nibiping'eni kuti nitenge namba yanu	I'm thirsty	Nimvela njota
		Open the window	Segulanikoni *window*
Can I drop you back at your place?	Nikupelekeni kunyumba kwanu?	Close the door	Vala *door* / Valani ku *door*
		Lock the door	Komani *door*
Let's go to my place	Tiye kunyumba kwanga	Turn on the light	Yashani *light*
I'm going to cook	Niyenda kupika	Turn up the volume	Ikanikoni *volume*
I'm going to wash the dishes	Niyenda kusuka mbale	Turn down the volume	Chosanikoni *volume*
Go and buy me some mobile phone credit	Kanigulilenikoni *talk time*	You look nice this evening	Koma uwoneka bwino lelo
		You look like someone I know	Wapalana na muntu wamene niziβa
Hold this for me	Nigwililenikoni ichi	I love you	Nikukonda
Just throw it away	Chitayeni	I'll miss you	Nizakuyewa

Emergencies

Help me!	Nitandizeni!
Is there someone who can help me?	Kuli wamene anganitandize?
Come quickly	Mubwele mwamusanga-musanga
It's an emergency	Ni *emergency*
What's happened?	Nichani chachitika?
There's been an accident	Kwachitika *accident*
There's been a fire	Kwachitika mulilo
I'm calling the police	Nizaitana βa *police*
Where is the nearest police station?	Nanga *police* yapafupi ili kuti?
Leave me alone!	Nisiyeni!
Don't touch me!	Osanigwila!
Go away!	Choka apa!
Thief!	Kawalala uyo!
They've stolen my money	βanibela ndalama
I haven't done anything wrong	Sininapange mulandu ulionse
Where are you taking me?	Nanga munipeleka kuti?
I want to talk to a lawyer	Nifuna kukamba na βa *lawyer*
Can I just pay a fine now?	Ningalipile ndalama manje?
How can we sort this out?	Tizasiliza bwanji vuto iyi?
I've lost...	Nasoβesa...
I left it in my room	Nenze naisiya mu *room* yanga
I feel ill	Nimvela kudwala
I had a fall	Nenze nagwa
I've been stung / bitten by...	Nalumiwa na...
I need a doctor	Nifuna βa *doctor*
Take me to the clinic	Nipelekeni ku *clinic*
It hurts here	Paβaβa apa
I'm bleeding	Nichoka magazi
I have a cough	Nili na chifuβa
I have a fever	Nili na *fever*
I've been injured	Nazichita
I'm pregnant	Nili na mimba
I'm already taking medication	Ninayamba kudala kumwa mankwala
I can't sleep	Nikangiwa kugona
I'm feeling worse	Nimvela kuipa maningi
I'm feeling better	Nimvelako bwino

English-Nyanja vocabulary

In this list, verb roots and other words that usually have a prefix attached are preceded with a dash (-). Traditional words that are widely known but have largely fallen out of use among speakers of Town Nyanja are labelled as "deep". Loanwords that are written with English spelling are shown in *italics*.

above · pamwamba [pa]
accident · *accident*, ngozi (deep)
accuse · -namizila
ache (v.) · -βaβa
admire · -kumbwila
adultery · chigololo
aeroplane · ndeke
be *afraid* · -yopa
again · futi
agree · -vomekeza
ahead · kusogolo
air · mpepo
alert (make aware) · -chenjeza
be *alive* · -nkala moyo
all · -onse (page 25)
allow · -vomeleza
already · kudala
always · lionse, ntawi zonse
and · na
angel · mungeli
anger (make angry) · -kwiyisa
be *angry* · -kalipa, -kwiya
animal · nyama (same as "meat")
answer (n.) · *answer*, yanko (deep)
answer (v.) · -yanka
ant · [ka]nyelele (common), mpasi (biting red ant), nyakapelele (flying ant)
apply (lotion) · -zola
argue · -shunshana
arm · kwanja (plural: *manja*)
arrest · -manga, -gwila (same as "hold")

arrive · -fika
around (a place or time) · ku (page 16)
as (like) · monga
ashes · milota
ask · -funsa (ask question), -pempa (ask for something)
at · pa, ku (see page 16)
aunt · [βa] *aunt* (some aunts are addressed using words for mother)
avocado · kotapela
be *awake* · -nkala menso
axe · katemo

baby · *baby*, bebi
back (of body) · musana
be *bad* · -ipa
bag · chola
baggage · katundu
ball · bola
banana · *banana*
baobab · muβuyu (tree), chiβuyu (fruit)
basket · *basket*, basiketi
bathe · -samba
be · -li, -nkala (page 24)
bean leaves · chimpapila
beans · binzi, nyemba
beard · ndevu
beat · -menya (hit), -tunta, -chaya (heartbeat)
because · chifukwa, ndaβa

become · -nkala
bed · *bed*, bedi
bed bugs · nsanya
bee · nzimu
beer · moβa
before · pambuyo
begin · -yamba
believe · -kulupilila, -biliva
believe in · -chetekela
belly · mimba, mala
belt · *belt*, belti
bend · -benda, -bendesa
bend over · -βelama
bewitch · -lowa
bicycle · njinga
big · -kulu
bird · nyoni
birth · kubadwa
bite · -luma
be bitter · -lula
bitterness · chikonko
black · *black*
blackjack (vegetable) · kanunka
blanket · *blanket*
blessings · madaliso
blind · -mpofu
block (n.) · *block*, buloko
block (v.) · -vala
blood · magazi
blow on · -fuzilila
blue · *blue*
board · *board*, bodi
boat · *boat*, boti
body · tupi
bogey · chimina

boil (v.) · -boila, -βila, -βilisa
bone · bonzo, munga (of fish)
bonus · mbasela
book · *book*, buku
boots · majombo
boredom · ulesi (same as "laziness")
be born · -badwa
borrow · -bweleka, -pempa (ask for)
bother (v.) · -vuta, -shupa
bottle · *bottle*, botolo
bottom · nyansi (of thing), matako (buttocks)
bowl · bowl
box · *box*, bokosi
boy · [ka]mwamuna ("little man"), munyamata (deep)
bracelet · kabango ("bangle")
brasier · mbaula
bread · *bread*, buledi
break · -ononga (damage), -pwanyika (smash), -tyola (snap), -tula (make a hole in)
breakfast · *breakfast*
breastfeed · -nyonka, -nyonsha
breasts · maβele, maziβa
breathe · -pema
breathlessness · befu
bridge · *bridge*
be bright (light) · -tuβa, -yakisa
bring · -leta
brother (or sister) · mukulu (older), mufana (younger)
brother-in-law · mulamu
brotherhood · chibale

be broken · -onongeka (damaged), -pwanyika (smashed), -tyoka (snapped), -tulika (leaky)
broom · chipyango
brown · *brown*
brush (teeth) · -suka
bucket · baketi
bug · kadoyo
build · -manga
bump · -bunka
burn · -pya (be hot), -ocha (incinerate), -shoka (scorch)
burp (v.) · -byola
bury · -fwikila (thing), -shika (person)
bus · *bus*, basi
bus stop · *bus stop*
busy · *busy*
but · koma, bati
butter · *butter*
butterfly · *butterfly*
buttocks · matako
buy · -gula

cabbage · *cabbage*, kabeji
cake · *cake*, keke
call · -ita (summon), -tuma (phone)
can (tin) · kakopo
candle · *candle*, kandulo
car · motoka
care for · -sunga (child), -dwazika (sick person), -onela (possession)
carrot · *carrot*, kaloti
carry · -nyamula, -papa (on back), -twika (on head)
carve · -bezela, -sema
cassava · kalundwe, tute

cassava leaves (food) · katapa
cat · pusi
catch · -gwila (ball), -yambula (disease)
caterpillar · *caterpillar*, chinkuβala (edible kind)
cattle · ng'ombe
cause (v.) · -lengesa
cease · -leka
celebration · pwando, madyelelo, chisangalalo
chair · mupando
chameleon · lumvwi
change (n.) · *change*
change (v.) · -chinja
charcoal · malasha
chase · -pilikisha
chase away · -pisha
chat (v.) · -cheza
be cheap · -chipa
check · -cheking'a
cheek · mbovu
chest (body part) · pachifuβa
chew · -sheta
chicken · nkuku
chief · mfumu
child · mwana (plural: βana)
chilli pepper · mpilimpili
chin · kalefulefu (Bemba)
choke · -kola
choose · -sanka
chop · -tema
Christmas · *Christmas*, Kirisimasi
church · *church*, chalichi
clap (hands) · -tota
class · *class*, kilasi
claw · njala (same as "fingernail")

be clean · -kilini, -tuβa
clean · -kilina
be clear (transparent) · -ngweleβela
be clever · -chenjela
click (press a button) · -tinika
climb · -kwela
clinic · *clinic*, chipatala
clock · *clock*, nkoloko
close (nearby) · pafupi
close (shut) · -vala
cloth · kanyula
clothes · vovala
clouds · makumbi
cockroach · *cockroach*
be cold · -zizila
cold (illness) · chinfine
colour · *colour*
comb (n.) · chisakulo
comb (v.) · -sakula
come · -bwela
come back · -bwelela
come from · -chokela
come out · -choka
compare · -linganiza
complain · -dandaula
be complete · -kwana
complete · -kwanisa
computer · *computer*, kompyuta
confusion · kusokonezeka
container · chigubu
continue · -pitiliza
cook · -pika
cooking stick · mutiko
copy · -kopeleza, -kopela (in a test)
corpse · chitumbi

corral (pen for livestock) · kola
cotton · *cotton*
cotton wool · tonje
cough · -kosomola
count · -penda
country · ziko
cousin · *cousin* (some cousins are addressed as brothers or sisters)
cover (v.) · -yambata (with sheet), -vala (with lid)
cow · ng'ombe
cowpea leaves · kachesha
crawl · -kalaβa
be crazy · -funta
create · -lenga
crocodile · ng'wena
crooked legs · matewe
cross (crucifix) · mutanda
cross over · -jumpa, -tauka
crow (bird) · chikwalakwala
be crowded · -pampa ("pumped")
crush · -pwanya
be crushed · -pwanyika
cry · -lila
cultivate (crops) · -lima
cup · *cup*
cut · -dula (cut through), -juβa (cut into)

damage · -ononga
dance (v.) · -vina
be dark · -fipa
darkness · mudima
daughter · mwana [mukazi]
daughter-in-law · mupongozi, βapongozi (respectful)
day · siku, *day*

daytime · muzuβa
death · imfa
debt · nkongole
defecate · -nya
deliberately · dala
demolish · -gumula
demon · chiβanda
depend on · -chetekela
descend · -seluka
describe · -shimika, -londolola
diaper · daipa, teβela (cloth diaper), chikwesa (plastic layer put on top)
diarrhoea · kutulula
die · -fa
differ · -siyana
be difficult · -vuta
dig · -kumba
be dim-witted · -pwalala, -shishita
dinner · sapa ("supper")
dirt · doti
be dirty · -fipa
disease · matenda
divide up · -gaβanisa, -gomola
do · -chita
doctor · [βa] *doctor*
dog · imbwa, galu (deep)
donkey · *donkey*
door · *door*
dove · nkunda
down (on the ground) · pansi
dragonfly · bembelezi
draw (picture) · -diloing'a
dream (n.) · chiloto, maloto
dream (v.) · -lota
dress (n.) · *dress*
dress (v.) · -vala, -valika

drink (v.) · -mwa
drip (be leaking) · -donya
drive · -yenza
drop (of water) · kadonya
drop (v.) · -gwesa
drum (instrument) · ngoma
be drunk (intoxicated) · -kolewa
be dry · -yuma
dry · -nyumika, -pukuta (wipe)
duck (n.) · *ducks* (often ends with -s even when singular), mbata (deep)
be dull (dim-witted) · -pwalala, -shishita
dump (for rubbish) · chishala
during · pantawi ya
dust · *dust*

eagle · *eagle*
ear · kwatu (plural: *matu*)
early morning · kuseniseni
earrings · masikiyo
Easter · *Easter*
be easy · *simple*
easily · mwamusanga
eat · -dya, -dyela (have a meal)
edge · pambali, pa *last*
egg · *egg*
egret · nkowa
elbow · kamboyo
electricity · ma *light*, malaiti
elephant · njovu
embarrass · -sebanya
be embarrassed · -sebanyika
end (v.) · -sila
be engaged (to marry) · -koβekela
English (language) · Chizungu
enter (go in) · -ngena

envy (v.) · -kumbwa, -kumbwila
epilepsy · kunyu
equal · -lingana
escape · -taβa
escort (v.) · -pelekeza
especially · makamaka
evening · mumazulo
everywhere · ponse, konse (page 26)
explain · -shimika, -londolola
extinguish · -zimya
eye · linso (plural: *menso*)
eyelashes, eyebrows · nsiye

face · pamenso, mfeshi
fade · -jujuka
faeces · matuvi
fail · -kangiwa
faint (pass out) · -fenta
fall · -gwa
familiar · -ziβika
family · *family*, banja (deep)
far away · kutali
farm · *farm*, famu
fart (n.) · chishupu
fart (v.) · -shula, -nya chisupu
fast · *fast*, mwamusanga
fasten · -manga
be fat (plump) · -ina
father · βatate, mudala (slang)
father-in-law · βapongozi
fear (v.) · -yopa
feast · pwando
feather · pepe
feel · -mva, -mvela (same as "hear")
feet · mendo

field (cultivated) · munda
be fierce · -kali
fig tree · mukuyu
fight (n.) · ndeo
fight (v.) · -menyana
fill up · -zulisa
find · -peza
finger · chikumo, kakumo, chimbombo
finish (complete) · -siliza
be finished · -sila
fire · mulilo, chimbilimbili (communal fire)
first (1st) · *number one* (page 13)
fish · nsomba
fit (have an epileptic fit) · -kunyuka
five · *five*
be flat (tyre) · -pompoloka, -poncha
flip (overturn) · -beuka, -beula
flour · *flour*, unga (maize meal)
flower · *flower*
fly (insect) · inzi
fly (v.) · -mbululuka
follow · -konka
food · chakudya, vakudya
fool · opusa, chisilu, chipuβa
be foolish · -pusa
foolishness · upuβa
foot · kwendo (plural: *mendo*)
footprint · chidindo
for · see page 23
forehead · mpumi
forest · [ku]sanga, [mu]sanga
forget · -iβala
forgive · -kululukila
forward · pasogolo

four · four
free · free
fresh · fresh
friend · bwenzi, munza- (page 14)
frighten · -yofya
fritter · chitumbuwa
frog · chule
front · kusogolo
fruit · fruit
fry · -fulaying'a, -kazinga
be full · -zula (container), -kuta (after eating)
fun · -sekesa
funeral · malilo
fur · masako

game (for playing) · game, gemu
garbage · doti
garden · garden, munda (field)
gather up · -kolola
gate · gate, geti
get off (bus) · -seluka
get on (bus) · -kwela
get up · -ima
get used to · -jaila
gift · gift, present, mpaso
giraffe · giraffe
girl · [ka]mukazi ("little woman"), gelo, musikana (deep), kampopo (slang)
give · -pasa
give birth · -bala
glass · glass
glasses · magogo ("goggles")
go · -yenda, -pita
go round · -zunguluka
goat · mbuzi

God · Mulungu
be good · -bwino, -mushe
gossip · -tonja
grade (at school) · grade
granadilla · gologodela
grandchild · muzukulu
grandfather · βambuya [βamuna], βashikulu (from Bemba)
grandmother · βambuya [βakazi]
grass · mauzu, kapinga (ornamental)
grasshopper · kantete (small), sontwa (big and green), chidiza (big and brown)
grave · manda
green · green
greet · -posha, -pasa moni
grey · grey
ground · pansi (down), [ma]doti (soil)
groundnuts · nshaβa
group · group, gulu
grow (cultivate) · -shanga
grow (get bigger) · -kula (person), -mela (plant, hair)
grow old · -kota
guard (n.) · guard, kamulonda
guard (v.) · -londa
guess · -lotela
guest · mulendo
guinea fowl · nkanga
gums · viponshi, ma gums
gun · mfuti

hair · sisi (on head), masako (fur)
hammer (n.) · sando
hammer (v.) · -kokomela
hand · kwanja (plural: manja)
hand over · -peleka

hang (swing) · -peluka
hang up · -yanika, -koloβeka, -koβeka (from Bemba)
happiness · chimwemwe
be happy · -kondwela
be hard (firm) · -kosa
hare · kalulu
hat · kasote, ndazo (slang)
hate (v.) · -zonda
have · -nkala na (page 24)
head · mutu (plural: *mitu*)
headscarf · chitambala
heal · -pola, -polesa
health · umoyo, ntanzi (deep)
heap · *heap*, hipu
hear · -mva, -mvela
heart · mutima
heat up · -pyesa (make hot), -fundisa, -tumisa (warm up)
Heaven · Kumwamba
heavy · -lema
hello · bwanji (page 31), odi (when entering a building)
help (n.) · tandizo
help (v.) · -tandiza
her (person) · eve (page 16)
her (possession) · yake, wake, etc (page 14)
heron · nkowa
hiccups · mundikundiku
hide (oneself) · -bisama
hide (something) · -bisa
hide-and-seek · chidunune, kabishabisha (from Bemba)
high (up) · mumwamba
hill · lupili, chulu

him · eve (page 16)
hippo · *hippo*
his · yake, wake, etc (page 14)
hit · -menya
hoe (n.) · kambwili
hold · -gwila
hole · mugodi (pit), kapunda (hole in something), chigamba (hole in clothing)
honey · uchi
hoof · chimbombo
hook · [ka]ndoβo
hop · -jentuka
horn · nsengo
horse · *horse*
hospital · *hospital*, chipatala
be hot · -pya, -tuma (warmed up)
hotel · *hotel*
house · nyumba
how many? · -ngati? (page 25)
how? · bwanji (page 25)
hug · -kumbatila
hundred · *hundred*
hunger · njala
hurry · -yendesa
hurt · -βaβa, -βaβisa
hyena · chimbwi

ice · *ice*
idiot · opusa, chisilu, chipuβa
if · ngati (page 30)
be ill (sick) · -dwala
illness · matenda
imprint (n.) · chidindo
imprint (v.) · -dinda
in · mu (page 16)
increase (grow) · -kwela

increase (raise prices) · -ikila
inform · -chenjeza
inhale · -pepa
insect · *insect*, kadoyo
inside · mukati
insult (v.) · -tukwana
intelligence · nzelu
interesting · wamizana
intestines · matumbo
introduce · -ziβisa
invent · -panga
investigate · -fufuza
iron (for clothes) · nsimbi
iron (v.) · -chisa
it · yeve, weve, etc (page 26)
be *itchy* · -nyeleza

jealousy · *jealous*, kalijo
job · nchito
join · -joina
journey · ulendo
juice · *juice*
jump · -jumpa
justice · chilungamo

keep · -gwililila, -mangilila (hold in place), -sunga (take care of)
kettle · *kettle*, ketulo
key · *key*, ki
kick (v.) · -chaya chibaka
kill · -paya
kind (type of thing) · mutundu
kindness · chifundo
kiss · -kising'a
knee · nkokola
kneel · -gwada

knife · *knife*
knit · -tunga
knock · -konkosha
knock off (from work) · -komboka
know · -ziβa

lake · *lake*
lamb · mbelele
language · chitundu
last (final) · *last*
be *late* (delayed) · -chedwa
laugh · -seka
laziness · ulesi
lead · -langiza
leak · -tulika (be broken), -donya (drip)
leaf · tepo
be *lean* · -yonda
lean (tilt) · -samila
learn · -punzila
leave · -siya (leave behind), -yenda (go)
left (side) · *left*
leg · kwendo (plural: *mendo*)
lemon · *lemon*
leopard · *leopard*
lesson · punzilo
letter (document) · kalata
letter (in alphabet) · leta, lembo (deep)
lice · inda
lick · -myanguta
lie (tell lies) · -nama
lie (untruth) · boza
lie down · -gona (same as "sleep")
life · umoyo
lift (v.) · -imya (raise), -nyamula (carry)
light (a fire) · -yasha

light (source of illumination) · *light*
lightning · kaleza, tuleza
lightweight · -pepuka
like (as) · monga
like (be attracted to) · -konda
likewise · chimozimozi
limp · -sunta
line · laini, mulaini
lion · nkalamu
lip · mulomo
listen · -mvela
little · pang'ono
live (v.) · -nkala (stay in a place), -nkala moyo (be alive)
be lively · -chenjelesa
lizard · *lizard*, buluzi
lock · -koma
long · -tali
look · -yangana
look after · -samalila, -yanganila, -onela
look for · -sakila
be loose (not fit well) · -sensela
lorry · *lorry*, lole
lose · -soβesa
be lost · -soβa
lotion · mafuta (same as "oil")
louse · inda
love (n.) · chikondi
love (v.) · -konda
loved one · okondewa
luck · mwayi
luggage · katundu
lunch · *lunch*

be mad (crazy) · -funta
maggot · chikusi
mango · *mango*
maize · milisi
make · -panga
malaria · *malaria*
man · mwamuna
many · -mbili
march (v.) · -maching'a
marijuana · chamba
market · *market*, maketi
marriage · chikwati
be married · -kwatiliwa
marry · -kwatila
massage (v.) · -china
mat · mpasa
match up · -linganiza
matches · *matches*, machisa (deep)
me · ine (page 16)
mealie meal · unga
mean (signify) · -tantauza
measure · -pima
meat · nyama (same as "animal")
medicine · mankwala
meeting · *meeting*
melt · -sungunula
be melted · -sungunuka
member · *member*, membala
men · βamuna (singular: *mwamuna*)
metal · nsimbi
middle · pakati
milk · *milk*, meleki
mill (n.) · chigayo
mill (v.) · -gaya
millipede · chongololo

mind (intelligence) · nzelu
miracle · *miracle*
mirror · *mirror*
miss · -misa (fail to reach), -yewa (regret absence)
be *missing* · -soβa
mistake · *mistake*
mix up · -sankaniza
be *mixed up* · -sankanizika
mole rat · mfuko
moment (of time) · kantawi
money · ndalama
monkey · kolwe
month · *month*
moon · mwezi
moonshine (illicit liquor) · kachasu
mop (n.) · chikolopo
mop (v.) · -kolopa
morning · kuseni
mortar (for grinding) · kabende
mosquito · *mosquito*
mother · muzimai, βamai (respectful)
mother-in-law · βapongozi
motorbike · honda
mould (for brick-making) · chikombola
mould (v.) · -umba, -βumba (from Bemba)
mountain · lupili, chulu
mouse · mbeβa
mousetrap · kapama
move (oneself) · -kuka, -fendela (short distance), -nyang'anya (shake)
move (something) · -fendeza
mucus · mamina
mud · matika
munch · -kokota

mushroom · bowa
mutter · -ng'ung'uzila
my · yanga, wanga, etc (page 14)

nail (fingernail) · njala
nail (for construction) · muspikili
nakedness · chintako
name (n.) · zina
nappy · daipa, teβela (cloth nappy), chikwesa (plastic layer put on top)
navel · mukombo
near · pafupi
neck · mukosi
need · -funika
needle · nyeleti
nest · [ka]nchisa
net · *net*
be *new* · *new*, -nyowani
news · *news*
night · usiku
nipple · katiti
no · iyayi, awe (from Bemba)
noise · chongo
normal · *normal*
nose · mpuno
now · manje
nshima · nsima
number · *number*, namba
nurse · *nurse*, nasi

be *off* (light) · -zima
offal · ma *offals*, chifu
oil · saladi (cooking oil), mafuta
okra · delele
be *old* (person) · -kota
old person · nkote

older sibling · mukulu
on (preposition) · pa (page 16)
be on (light) · -yaka
once · kamozi (page 13)
once upon a time · panali panali
one · -mozi (page 13)
onion · *onion*, onyoni
open · -vula, -segula
or · olo
orange · *orange*
orphan · mwana wamasiye
our · yatu, watu, etc (page 14)
outside · panja
oven · oven
be overcooked · -pyesa
overturn · -beuka, -beula (flip), -pindamuka, -pindamula (turn over)
owl · kazizi
owner · mwine (plural: βene)

pack · -paking'a, -longa
pain · kuβaβa
paint (n.) · *paint*
paint (v.) · -penta
pants · bamba (underwear), kabudula (shorts), trauzi, toloshi (trousers)
paper · *paper*, pepa
parents · makolo
park (car) · -paking'a
part · *part*, nsimbi (car part)
party (celebration) · *party*, madyelelo
pastor · βabusa
path · njila
pay · -lipila
peace · mutendele
peach · piches

peanuts · nshaβa
pedal (v.) · -chova
peek at · -sonjelela
peel (n.) · chikamba
peel (v.) · -shuβa (with fingers), -pala (with knife)
peg · *pegs* (often ends with -s even when singular), pegezi
pencil · *pencil*, penso
penis · mbolo
people · βantu
perhaps · kapena
person · muntu
pick up · -doba
picture · *picture*, pikicha
pierce · -lasa
pig · nkumba
pineapple · *pineapple*, chinanazi
pile · chulu ("mountain")
pink · *pink*
pipe · *pipe*
pit · mugodi (same as "well")
pity · chifundo
place · malo
plait · -manga (same as "tie")
plank · pulanga
plane (aeroplane) · ndeke
plant (v.) · -shanga
plastic · *plastic*
plate · mbale
play · -soβela (children), -teya (game), -liza (instrument), -chaya bola (football)
plead · -papata
please (v.) · -kondwelesa
plenty · -chuluka
plot (of land) · *plot*

pocket · tumba
point at · -sonta
poison · *poison*
poke · -twinga
police, policeman · βakapokola, [βa] *police*
polish (v.) · -polisha
be poor · -sauka
popcorn · mapopukoni
porridge · *porridge*, poreji
possess · -nkala na (page 24)
potato · *potato*
pot · poto
pound · -twa
pounding stick · kamusi
pour · -tila
power · mpamvu (strength), malaiti (electricity)
pray · -pempela
prayer · pempelo
preach · -lalikila
be pregnant · -nkala na mimba
prepare (oneself) · -konzekela
present · *present, gift*, mpaso
press · -tinika
pretend · -vipanga, -ichaila
prevent · -chingiliza
previously · kudala
price · mutengo
prick · -lasa, -twinga
print (n.) · chidindo
prison · jele ("jail")
problem · vuto
promiscuity · chiwerewere
pronounce · -chulila
prostitute · hule

protect · -chingiliza
be proud · -zimvesa
province · *province*
pubic hair · [ma]vuzi
pull · -donsa
pump · *pump*
pumpkin · *pumpkin*, chitanje
pumpkin leaves · chiβwaβwa
punch (n., with fist) · kofi
punch (v.) · -chaya kofi
punish · -panisha
push · -pushing'a
put · -ika, -faka
put up · -imya

quarrel · -yambana
question · funso
quickly · *fast*, mwamusanga
quiet (n.) · zii

rabbit · kalulu
rage · chifukushi
railway · njanji
rain (n.) · mvula
rain (v.) · -loka (*mvula iloka* "it rains")
rainbow · *rainbow*
rape (v.) · -reping'a
rat · koswe
be raw (uncooked) · -βisi
reach (arrive at a destination) · -fika
read · -βelenga
be ready · -konzeka
receive · -pokelela
red · *red*
relative (family member) · bululu

remain · -sala
remember · -kumbuka
remind · -kumbusa
remove · -chosa
repeat · -bwezela
rescue · -pulumusa
respect (n.) · ulemu
respect (v.) · -lemekeza
rest · -pumula
return (come back) · -bwelela
reveal · -ulula
rhino · rhino
rice · rice
ride · -yendela pa
be right (correct) · -lunga
right (side) · right
rinse · -sukuluza
ripe · -pya
ripen (make ripe) · -pyesa, -vundika
rise (sun) · -choka
river · mumana
road · road, museβo (from Bemba)
roast · -ocha, -shoka
rock · mwala (plural: *miyala*)
roof · mutenge
roofing sheet · lilata (plural: malata)
room · room
root · muzyu
rope · ntambo
rot · -ola
be rough · -kalaβana
round · round, -laundi
rub · -zola
rubbish · doti
rules · malamulo

run · -tamanga
run away · -taβa

sack · sack, saka
be sad · -kalipa (same as "angry")
saliva · mata
salt · salt
sand · sand
sarong · chitenge
save (rescue) · -pulumusa
say · -kamba
scald · -fyunduka
scatter · -salanganya
be scattered · -salangana
school · school, sikulu
score (goal) · -ngenesa
scratch (v.) · -nyaula, -kwesha
scratch off · -kweshula
screw (v.) · -manga (same as "tie")
scrub (n.) · chifuso (for dishes), chisaka (for body)
scrub (v.) · -geza (body), -kwesha (thing), -suka (dishes)
search · -sakila
second (2nd) · *number two* (page 13)
secret · secret, sikiliti
see · -ona
seed · nsele
sell · -gulisa
send · -tuma
servant · wanchito
set (put) · -ika, -faka
set (sun) · -ngena ("go in")
sew · -tunga
shade · chimfwile
shadow · chimvwilimvwili

shake (something) · -nyang'anya
share (v.) · -gaβanisa
be sharp · -twa
shave · -gela
shawl · shawelo
shine (be bright) · -sanika
be shiny · -βeka
shirt · shirt
shiver · -tutuma
shoes · nsapato
shoot (v.) · -shuta
shop · shop, *shopo*
short · -fupi
shorts · kabudula
shoulder · shoulder, pewa
should (need to) · -funika
should have · sembe (page 22)
shout · -punda
show · -onesa (reveal), -sonyeza (point at)
shut · -vala
be sick · -dwala (be unwell), -luka (vomit)
sickness · matenda
side · mumbali, *side*, saidi
sieve · sefa
sign · *sign*, saini
similar · -palana
sin (n.) · chimo
sin (v.) · -chimwa
since · kuchokela ("coming from")
sing · -yimba
sister (or brother) · mukulu (older), mufana (younger)
sister-in-law · mulamu
sit · -nkala [pansi]

size · *size*, saizi
skin · nkanda
skipping rope · -chikwampe
skull · lukoβo
sky · kumwamba
slash (grass) · -kwapa
slasher · chikwakwa
slave · kapolo
sleep (n.) · tulo
sleep (v.) · -gona
slip · -teleleka
be slippery · -telela
slowly · pang'ono-pang'ono
be small · -chepa, -ng'ono
smash · -pwanya
be smashed · -pwanyika
smell (n.) · [ka]fungo
smell (v.) · -nunka
smile · -sekelela
smoke (n.) · chusi
smoke (tobacco) · -bema fwaka, -pepa fwaka
be smooth · -telela (slippery), -teka (soft)
snail · [chi]nkonono
snake · njoka
sneak · -βenda
sneeze · -yentyemula
snore (v.) · -liza minkonono
snot · mamina
so · *so*
soap · sopo
be soft · -teka
soil · [ma]doti ("dirt")
something · chintu, kantu
sometimes · ntawi zina

son · mwana [mwamuna]
son-in-law · mupongozi, βapongozi (respectful)
song · nyimbo
soon · manje manje
sore (open wound) · chilonda
be sore · -βaβa
soul · muzimu
sound · *sound*
soup · supu
be sour · -lula (same as "bitter")
speak · -kamba
spear · *spear*
spectacles · magogo ("goggles")
spider · *spider*
spinach · *spinach*
spirit · muzimu
spit (n.) · mata
spit (v.) · -tunya
spoil · -ononga
sponge (n.) · chifuso (for dishes), chisaka (for body)
spoon · *spoon*
squash (v.) · -pwanya
be squashed · -pwanyika
squeeze · -fyanta
stab · -lasa
stamp (make an imprint) · -dinda
stand · -ima, -imilila, -nyamuka
star · *star*, nyenyezi (deep)
start · -yamba, -liza (engine)
steal · -ba
steam · *steam*, stimu
step on · -dyaka
stick (of wood) · kamutengo
stick on · -mamatila

stick together · -matika
be stiff · -kosa
sting · -luma (same as "bite")
stink · -nunka
stir · -vundula
stomach · mumala
stone (in fruit) · chinshele
stone (rock) · mwala (plural: *miyala*)
stop · -leka (cease), -imilila (stand still)
story · kashimi
stove · *stove*, stovu
be straight · *straight*, -ongoka (deep)
straighten · -yondolola
be strange · -dabwisa
strangle · -kama
stream · ka *stream*, kamumana
strength · mpamvu
strengthen · -limbisa
stretch · -yondoloka, -yondolola
strike (hit) · -menya
string · kantambo
be strong · -limba, -nkala na mpamvu
be stupid · -pusa (foolish), -pwalala, -shishita (dim-witted)
such-and-such · chakuti-chakuti
suckle · -nyonka, -nyonsha
sugar · *sugar*
sugar cane · musale
sun · [ka]zuβa
sunflower · *sunflower*
be sure · -simikiza
be surprised · -dabwa
swallow (bird) · kamimbya
swallow (v.) · -mela
swear at · -tukwana
sweat (n.) · chiβe

sweat (v.) · -piβa
sweep · -pyanga
be *sweet* · *sweet*, -nzuna
sweet potato · kandolo
sweet potato leaves · kalembula
swell (v.) · -vimba
swim · -nyaya
swing (n.) · mupelu
swing on · -peluka
switch on (light) · -yasha
switch off (light) · -zimya

table · *table*
tail · muchila
take · -tenga
take a picture · -kopa
take away · -chosa
take off (clothes) · -vula
talk · -kamba
tap · *tap*, pompi
tax · *tax*, musonko (deep)
teach · -punzisa
teacher · [βa] *teacher*, [βa]ticha
tear · -ng'amba
tears (from crying) · misozi
teeth · meno
telephone · foni
tell · -uza
temptation · mayeso (same as "trials")
ten · *ten*, teni
term · *term*, temu
testicles · machende, mapolo
thank · -yamika, -onga (deep), -tasha (from Bemba)
thank you · zikomo
that (introducing a clause) · kuti

that (reporting speech) · ati
that (which) · chamene, etc (page 15)
their · yaβo, waβo, etc (page 14)
them · βeve, etc (page 16)
thief · kawalala
thigh · chiβelo
thing · chintu
think · -ganiza
third (3rd) · *number three* (page 13)
thirst · njota
thorn · munga
thoughts · maganizo
three · -tatu (page 13)
throat · pamukosi
throw · -ponya, -tema (missile)
throw away · -taya
throw up (vomit) · -luka
thumb · chikumo
thunder · tuleza
tidy · -wamya (make nice)
tie · -manga
tight · *tight*
tighten · -mangisa
time · ntawi (often shortened to *ntau*)
tin can · kakopo
be *tired* · -lema
to · ku (pages 16 & 18)
tobacco · fwaka
today · lelo
toe · kakumo [ka kumendo], chimbombo
together · pamozi
toilet · *toilet*, chimbuzi (deep)
tomato · *tomato*
tomorrow · mailo (same as "yesterday")
tongue · lulimi

tools · voseβenzesa
tooth · lino (plural: *meno*)
toothpaste · kolgeti ("Colgate")
be *torn* · -ng'ambika
tortoise · fulu
touch · -gwila
town · *town*, tauni
toy · *toy*, toyi
tradition · ntambi
trap (mousetrap) · kapama
tree · mutengo
trip (v.) · -zibuntula
trouble (n.) · vuto
trouble (v.) · -vuta, -shupa
be *troubled* · -vutika
trials · mayeso
tribe (of person) · mutundu
trotter · chimbombo
trousers · trauzi, toloshi (from Bemba)
trust (v.) · -chetekela
truth, truly · zoona
try · -yesa
turn (on road) · -koneka
turn around (oneself) · -pindamuka, -tembenuka
turn around (something) · -pindamula
twice · kaβili (page 13)
twin · mupundu
twist · -ponyongola
two · -βili (page 13)
type (kind of thing) · mutundu

umbrella · *umbrella*
uncle · [βa] *uncle* (some uncles are addressed using words for father)
be *uncooked* · -βisi

uncover · -vununkula
underneath · kunyansi
understand · -mvesa, -mwela
undress · -vula
unpack · -longolola
be *unripe* · -βisi
unable to · -lepela
untie · -mangusula
until · kufikila
unwind · -pombosola
be *unwound* · -pombosoka
up · pamwamba
be *upset* · -kalipa
upset · -kalipisa
urinate · -tunda
urine · mitundo
us · ise (page 16)
use · -seβenzesa

vagina · [ka]nini, kadanana
value · pindu
van · *van*
be *varied* · -siyana-siyana
vegetables (leafy greens) · maveji
very much · kwambili, maningi
village · munzi
visit (v.) · -tandala
visitor · mulendo
vomit (n.) · malusi
vomit (v.) · -luka
vote (v.) · -vota

wait for · -lindila, -yembekezela
wake (oneself) · -uka
wake (someone) · -usha

walking stick · nkoli
wall · chipupa, chiβumba (from Bemba)
want · -funa
war · nkondo
be *warm* · -funda, -tuma
warm up · -fundisa, -tumisa
wash · -washa (clothes), -suka (things)
washing line · ntambo ("rope")
wasp · mago
watch (v.) · -tamba
watchman · *guard*, kamulonda
water (n.) · manzi
water (v.) · -tilila
watermelon · *watermelon*
wave (v.) · -baibisha
way · njila
weak · -sakosa ("not strong"), -fooka (feel weak), -lefuka (tired)
wealth · chuma
weave · -tunga
week · *week*
weekend · *weekend*
welcome (v.) · -landila
well (for water) · mugodi
well (nicely) · bwino, mushe
be *wet* · -nana
what? · chani?
wheel · *wheel*, wilo
wheelbarrow · *wheelbarrow*, wilba
when (if) · ngati (page 30)
when? (question) · liti? (page 25)
when (while) · pamene
where? · kuti?, pati? (page 25)
which? (question) · iti?, uti?, chiti?, etc (page 25)

which (that) · yamene, wamene, chamene, etc (page 15)
whip (n.) · mukwapu
whip (v.) · -kwapula
whistle (n.) · kamfyoli
whistle (v.) · -liza kamfyoli
white · *white*
white person · muzungu
who · wamene (one who...), βamene (those who...)
who? (question) · [βa]ndani? (page 25)
whore · hule
why? · chifukwa [chani]?
wide · -kulu (same as "big")
wig · *wig*, wigi
win · -wina
wind (n.) · mpepo
wind (v.) · -pomba
wing · papiko
winnow · -pepeta
wipe (dry off) · -pukuta
wipe bottom · -pipa, -shinda
wire · *wire*
wisdom · nzelu
witch · mfwiti
witchcraft · umfwiti
witchdoctor · ng'anga
with · na
be *without* · -libe
woman · mukazi
wood · nkuni
word · *word*
work (n.) · nchito
work (v.) · -gwila nchito, -seβenza
world · ziko (same as "country")

worm · *worm,* munyongololo, njoka ya mumala (intestinal worm)
worry · -dandaula, -waling'a, -wala (slang)
wring (clothes) · -fina
wrinkles · mankwinya
write · -lemba
be **wrong** · -lakwa

yawn · -yaula
year · *year*
yellow · *yellow*
yes · ee
yesterday · mailo (same as "tomorrow")
you (singular) · iwe (page 16)
you (plural or respectful) · imwe (page 16)
younger sibling · mufana
your (singular) · yako, wako, etc
your (plural or respectful) · yanu, wanu, etc (page 14)

zebra · *zebra*

Nyanja-English vocabulary

Listed here are some of the most common words of Town Nyanja, excluding obvious English borrowings (for which no dictionary is needed). This list also includes words that originally come from other languages such as Bemba but are now widely known and used among Nyanja speakers. Verb roots and other words that usually have a prefix attached are preceded with a dash (-).

a- · he, she (subject prefix, page 19)
aβa · these (page 16)
aka · this (page 16)
apa, apo · here, there (page 16)
ati · [he/she said] that (page 30), what?
awe · no
aya · these (page 16)

-ba · steal
βa- · they, them – plural prefix or concord used for humans (noun class 2), also a marker of respect; see page 10
βa · of, belonging to (page 14)
-βaβa, -βaβisa · hurt
βabusa · pastor
badi · too much, very much ("badly")
-badwa · be born
-baibisha · wave
-bala · give birth
βamai · mother
βamalume · uncle (mother's brother)
bamba · underpants
βambuya · grandparents
βamene · those who (page 15)
βamuna · men (singular: *mwamuna*)
βana · children (singular: *mwana*)
βandani? · who? (plural or respectful)
βangati? · how many? (page 25)
βantu · people (singular: *muntu*)

βapongozi · father-in-law, mother-in-law, son-in-law, daughter-in-law
βashikulu · grandfather
basi · bus
βatate · father
bati · but
βati? · which people?, who? (page 29)
befu · breathlessness
-βeka · be shiny
βeka · by themselves (page 25)
-βelama · bend over
βele · breast
-βelenga · read
-bema fwaka · smoke
bembelezi · dragonfly
βena, βenangu · some of them, others (page 25)
-benda, -bendesa · bend
-βenda · sneak
βene · owners (singular: *mwine*)
βenze · they were (page 21)
-beuka, -beula · overturn, flip over, get rich (slang)
βeve · them (page 16)
-bezela · carve
-βila, -βilisa · boil (v.)
-βili · two (page 13)
binzi · beans
-bisa, -bisama · hide
-βisi · raw, unripe, uncooked

βo- · those who (page 15)
βoi · friend (term of address)
-boila · boil (v.), be angry (slang)
bokosi · box, buttocks (slang)
bola · ball, football
βonse · all of them (page 25)
bonzo · bone
boti · boat
bowa · mushroom
boza · lie, untruth
buledi · bread
bululu · relative, family member
buluzi · lizard
-βumba · mould (into shape)
-bundulila · steal a glance
-bunka · bump
-bunkisa · get into an accident, catch venereal disease (slang)
βushe · question marker (page 25)
bwanji? · how?, what kind?
-bwela · come
-bweleka · borrow
-bwelela · come back
bwenzi · friend
bwete · buttocks (slang)
-bwezela · repeat
-bwino · be good, well
-byola · burp

cha · of, belonging to (page 14)
chabe · only, just
chaka · year
chakudya · food
chakuti-chakuti · such-and-such
chamba · marijuana
chamene · that which (page 15)

chani? · what? (page 29)
-chaya bola · play football
-chaya chibaka · kick
-chaya kofi · punch
che · shortening of *chabe* or *chamene*
-chedwa · be late, delayed
-chenjela · be clever
-chenjelesa · be lively
-chenjeza · alert, inform
-chepa · be small
-chetekela · believe in, depend on
cheve · it (page 26)
-cheza · chat
chi- · singular prefix or concord used for a 'thing' or something big or bad (noun class 7); see page 10
chibaka · kick
chibale · brotherhood
chiβanda · demon
chiβe · sweat
chiβelo · thigh
chiβuku · maize beer ('opaque')
chibululu · family relationship
chiβumba · wall
chiβuyu · baobab fruit
chiβwaβwa · pumpkin leaves
chiβwantu · a thick maize drink
chidindo · imprint, footprint, stamp
chidiza · big brown grasshopper
chidunune · hide-and-seek
chifu · offal
chifukushi · rage
chifukwa · because, why
chifundo · kindness, mercy, pity
chifuso · scrub, sponge (for dishes)

chigamba · hole in clothing (plural: *magamba*)
chigayo · mill (for grinding corn)
chigololo · adultery
chigubu · container
chikaβaβula · an insect with itchy hairs
chikamba · peel (e.g. of banana)
chikolopo · mop
chikombola · mould (for brick-making)
chikondi · love
chikonko · bitterness
chikopo · empty can, dim-witted person (slang)
chikumo · thumb, big toe
chikusi · maggot
chikwakwa · slasher (for grass)
chikwalakwala · crow (bird)
chikwampe · skipping rope
chikwanga · layer of overcooked nshima at the bottom of the pot
chikwati · marriage
chikwesa · plastic layer over nappy/diaper
-chila · surpass (page 25)
chilanga mulilo · feast put on for new husband (nowadays often mixed with *mateβeto*)
chilango · punishment
chilendo · foreignness, strangeness
chiloto · dream
chilungamo · justice, fairness
chimbayambaya · useless old car
chimbilimbili · communal fire
chimbombo · finger, toe, hoof, trotter
chimbwi · hyena
chimfwile · shade

chimina · bogey, booger (nasal mucus)
chimo · sin (n.)
chimpapila · bean leaves
chimponda · roasted groundnut paste
chimvwilimvwili · shadow
-chimwa · commit sin
chimwemwe · happiness
-china · massage (v.)
china, chinangu · one of them, another (page 26)
chinfine · cold (illness)
-chingiliza · protect, prevent
-chinja · change
chinkuβala · edible caterpillar
chinshele · stone (in fruit)
chintako · nakedness
chintu · thing
Chinyanja · Nyanja language
-chipa · be cheap
chipamba · wooden tool for scooping nshima from the pot
chipatala · hospital, clinic
chipuβa · fool
chipupa · wall
chipyango · broom
-chisa · iron (v.)
chisaka · scrub, sponge (for body)
chisakulo · comb
chisangalalo · celebration
chishala · rubbish dump
chishupu · fart
chisilu · fool
-chita · do
chitambala · headscarf
chitanje · pumpkin
chitenje · sarong, traditional dress

chiti? · which one? (page 29)
chitumbi · corpse
chitumbuwa · 'fritter' (dough ball)
chitundu · language
chiwaya · dry maize kernels
chiwelewele · promiscuity
Chizungu · English language
cho- · that which (page 15)
-choka · come out, rise (sun)
-chokela · come from
chola · bag
chongo · noise
chongololo · millipede
chonse · all (page 26)
-chosa · remove, take away
-chova · pedal (v.)
chule · frog
-chulila · pronounce
chulu · hill, mountain, pile
-chuluka · be plenty
chuma · wealth
chusi · smoke

-dabwa · be surprised
-dabwisa · be strange
dala · deliberately, on purpose
-dandaula · complain, worry
delele · okra
-dendekela · balance something on one's head
-diloing'a · draw
-dinda · imprint (v.)
-doba · pick up
-doba mwana · have illegitimate child
-donsa · pull
-donya · drip, leak (v.)

doti · dirt, rubbish
-dula · cut through
-dwala · be ill, sick
-dwazika · care for (sick person)
-dya · eat
-dyaka · step on
-dyela · eat well, have a meal

ee · yes
eka · by himself/herself (page 25)
enze · he/she was (page 21)
eve · him, her (page 16)

-fa · die
-faka · put, set
-fendela, -fendeza · move
-fenta · faint, pass out
-fika · arrive
-fina · wring (clothes)
-fipa · be dark, dirty
-fola · get paid
foni · telephone
-fooka · feel weak
-fufuza · investigate
fulu · tortoise
-funa · want
-funda · be warm
-fundisa · warm up
fungo · smell
-funika · need
-funsa · ask (question)
funso · question
-funta · be crazy
-fupi · be short, near
futi · again

-fuzilila · blow on
fwaka · tobacco
-fwikila · bury
-fyanta · squeeze
-fyunduka · scald

-gaβanisa · share, divide up
-ganiza · think
-gaya · mill (grind corn)
-gela · shave
-geza · scrub (body), bathe (slang)
gologodela · granadilla (fruit)
-gomola · divide
-gona · sleep, lie down
gong'a · fake thing, ugly person
-gula · buy
-gulisa · sell
gulu · group
gumugumu · a big-headed lizard, big-headed person (slang)
-gumula · demolish
-gwa · fall
-gwada · kneel
-gwela · fall into
-gwesa · drop
-gwila · hold, touch, grab, arrest
-gwila nchito · work

hipu · heap
honda · motorbike
hule · whore

i- · it - concord used for a noun in class 5 or 9 (see page 10)
-iβala · forget
ichi · this (page 16)

-ika · put, set
-ikila · increase (raise price)
-ima · get up, stand up
-imba · sing
imbwa · dog
imfa · death
-imilila · stand
imwe · you (plural or respectful) (page 25)
impwa · a vegetable like a small yellow eggplant/aubergine
-imya · lift
-ina · be fat
ina, inangu · one of them, another (page 26)
inda · louse
ine · me (page 25)
inswa · edible flying termite
inzi · fly
-ipa · be bad
ise · us (page 25)
-ita · call, summon
ivi · these (page 16)
iti? · which one? (page 29)
iwe · you (singular) (page 25)
iyayi · no
iyi · this (page 16)
izi · these (page 16)

-jaila · get used to
jele · jail, prison
-jentuka · hop
-joina · join
-juβa · cut into
-jujuka · fade
-jumpa · jump, cross over

ka- · little – singular prefix/corcord used for a small thing (noun class 12); see page 10
ka · of, belonging to (page 14)
ka? · question marker (page 29)
kabango · bracelet
kabeji · cabbage
kabende · mortar (for grinding)
kabishabisha · hide-and-seek
kabudula · pants, shorts
kachasu · moonshine (illicit liquor)
kachesha · cowpea leaves
kadonya · drop (of water)
kadoyo · 'bug', insect, germ, HIV
kajilijili · sachet of cheap spirit
kakopo · tin can
kakumo · finger, toe
-kalaβa · crawl
-kalaβana · be rough
kalata · letter (document)
kalefulefu · chin
kalembula · sweet potato leaves
kaleza · lightning
-kali · bad, painful, fierce
kalijo · jealousy
-kalipa · be angry, upset
-kalipisa · anger, upset
kaloβa · money-lending with interest
kalulu · rabbit, hare
kalundwe · cassava
-kama · strangle, throttle
kamulonda · watchman
-kamba · speak
kamboyo · elbow
kambwili · hoe
kamfyoli · whistle

kamimbya · swallow (bird)
kampopo · pretty girl (slang)
kamusi · pounding stick
kamutengo · stick
kanchisa · nest
kandolo · sweet potato
-kangiwa · fail
kansi · nevertheless
kantambo · string
kantete · small grasshopper
kanunka · blackjack (vegetable)
kanyelele · ant
kanyula · cloth
kapama · mousetrap
kapena · perhaps
kapenta · tiny freshwater fish
kapinga · ornamental grass
kapolo · slave
kaponya · hawker, tout
kapunda · hole (in something)
kashimi · story
kasote · hat
katemo · axe
katiti · nipple
katundu · luggage, cargo
kawalala · thief
kaya · I wonder
-kazinga · fry
kazizi · owl
kazuβa · sun
keke · cake
kena, kenangu · one of them, another (page 26)
keve · it (page 26)
-kilina · clean
-kilini · be clean

-*koβeka* · hang up
-*koβekela* · get engaged
kofi · punch (n.)
-*kokomela* · hammer (v.)
-*kokota* · munch
kola · corral, pen for livestock
-*kola* · choke
-*kolewa* · drunk, intoxicated
kolgeti · toothpaste
kolo · parent
-*koloβeka* · hang up
-*kolola* · gather up
-*kolopa* · mop (v.)
kolwe · monkey
koma · but
-*koma* · lock
-*komboka* · knock off (from work)
-*konda* · love, like
-*kondwela* · be happy
-*kondwelesa* · please
-*koneka* · turn
-*konka* · follow
-*konkosha* · knock
konse · all, everywhere (page 26)
-*konzeka* · be ready
-*konzekela* · prepare (oneself)
-*kopa* · take a picture
-*kopeleza* · repeat, copy
-*kosa* · be strong, firm
-*kosomola* · cough
koswe · rat
-*kota* · grow old
kotapela · avocado
ku- (1) · to, at (locative prefix, page 16)
ku- (2) · prefix found on infinitive / noun forms of verbs (page 18)

ku- (3) · you (object prefix, page 19)
kudala · in the past, already
kuja · there (page 16)
-*kuka* · move
-*kula* · grow
kulibe · there isn't (page 16)
-*kulu* · be big
-*kululukila* · forgive
-*kulupilila* · believe
-*kumba* · dig
-*kumbwa, -kumbwila* · envy, admire
-*kumbatila* · hug
-*kumbuka* · remember
-*kumbusa* · remind
kunja · on the outside
kuno · here (page 16)
kunyu · epilepsy
-*kunyuka* · have a fit
kuseni · morning
kuseniseni · early morning
kusogolo · front, ahead
-*kuta* · be full (after eating)
kutali · far away
kuti (conjunction) · that
kuti? (question) · where? (page 25)
kwa · at the place of (page 16)
kwambili · very much
kwamene · at the place which (page 15)
-*kwana* · be complete, sane
-*kwanisa* · complete, put in place
kwanja · arm, hand
-*kwapa* · slash
-*kwapula* · whip
kwasila · enough, finished
-*kwatila* · marry

-kwatiliwa · be married
kwatu · ear (can also mean "our place")
-kwela · climb, get on (bus)
kwendo · leg, foot
-kwesha · scrub, scratch (thing)
-kweshula · scratch off
kweve · there, at that place (page 26)
kwinangu · somewhere else (page 26)
-kwiya · be angry

laini · line
-lakwa · be wrong
-lalikila · preach
-landila · welcome
-langiza · lead
-lasa · pierce, stab, prick
-lefuka · be weak, tired
-leka · cease, finish
lelo · today
-lema · be heavy, tired
-lemba · write
-lemekeza · respect, honour
-lenga · create
-lengesa · cause
-lepela · be unable to
-leta · bring
-li · be (page 24)
li- · singular prefix used for certain items in noun class 5; see page 10
-libe · be without (page 24)
-lila · cry, be running (engine)
lilasha · lump of charcoal (plural: *malasha*), pumice stone
lilata · roofing sheet (plural: *malata*)
-lima · farm, cultivate
-limba · be strong

-limbisa · strengthen
-linda · have an erection
-lindila · wait, wait for
ling'a · crack on foot (plural: *mang'a*)
-lingana · equal
-linganiza · match up, compare
lino · tooth (plural: *meno*)
linso · eye (plural: *menso*)
lionse · always
-lipila · pay
liti? · when?
-liza · play (instrument), make cry, start (engine)
loβola · bride price
-loka · rain
-londa · guard
-londolola · explain, describe
-longolola · unpack
-lota · dream
-lotela · guess
-lowa · bewitch
luβango · winnowing basket
-luka · vomit
lukoβo · skull
-lula · be bitter, sour
lulimi · tongue
-luma · bite, sting
lumanda · a vegetable
lumvwi · chameleon
-lunga · be right, correct
lupili · hill

m' · shortening of *mu-*

ma- · plural prefix used with a wide variety of items (noun class 6); corresponding singular forms occasionally begin with *li-* but usually have no prefix; see page 10

maβele · breasts
machende · testicles
madyelelo · party, celebration
mafulufute · type of insect that emerges after rain
mafuta · oil, lotion
magamba · holes in clothing
maganizo · thoughts
magazi · blood
mago · wasp
magogo · glasses, spectacles
mai · mother (respectful: *βamai*)
mailo · yesterday, tomorrow
majombo · boots
makamaka · especially
maketi · market
makolo · parents
makumbi · clouds
mala · belly
malamulo · rules
malasha · charcoal
malata · roofing sheets (singular: *lilata*)
malilo · funeral
malo · place
maloto · dreams
malukula · mortuary attendant
malume · uncle (mother's brother)
-mamatila · stick to
mami · term of address for a woman
mamina · snot, mucus
manda · grave, cemetery

mang'a · cracks on feet
-manga (1) · tie, plait, fasten, screw
-manga (2) · build
-mangisa · tighten, get arrested
-mangusula · unfasten, unscrew
mangwenu · missing tooth
maningi · very much
manja · arms, hands (singular: *kwanja*)
manje · now
manje manje · soon
mankwala · medicine, remedy
mankwinya · wrinkles
mantongo · gound (dirt in corner of eye)
manzi · water
mapolo · testicles
masako · fur
mashamo · continuous bad luck
masikiyo · earrings
maskuna · high-heeled shoes
mata · saliva, spittle
matako · buttocks
mateβeto · feast put on for husband
matenda · illness, disease
matewe · crooked legs
matika · mud
-matika · stick (v.)
matu · ears (singular: *kwatu*)
matumbo · intestines
matuvi · faeces
mauzu · grass
maveji · leafy green vegetables
mavuzi · pubic hair
mayeso · temptation, trials
maziβa · breasts
mbale · plate, dish

mbasela · bonus, extra
mbaula · brasier
mbeβa · mouse, bush rat
mbelele · lamb
-mbili · many
mbolo · penis
mbovu · cheek (side of face)
-mbululuka · fly (v.)
mbuyo · bottom
mbuzi · goat
-mela (1) · grow
-mela (2) · swallow
mendo · legs, feet (singular: *kwendo*)
meno · teeth (singular: *lino*)
menso · eyes (singular: *linso*)
-menya · hit, beat, fight with
mfeshi · face
mfuko · mole rat
mfumu · chief
mfuti · gun
mfwiti · witch
mi- · plural prefix used for long or wooden things (noun class 4); corresponding singular forms begin with *mu-*; see page 10
milisi · maize
milota · ashes
mimba · belly
-misa · miss, fail to hit
misozi · tears
mitundo · urine
moβa · beer
monga · as, like
moni · greeting
monse (1) · all of you (page 25)
monse (2) · in every place (page 26)
mosa- · don't (prohibition, page 28)
motoka · car
-mozi · one (page 13)
mpamvu · strength, power
mpasa · reed mat
mpasi · biting red ant
mpaso · gift, present
mpele · a skin disease
mpepo · air, wind
mpilimpili · chilli pepper
mpilu · a leafy vegetable
-mpofu · be blind
mpumi · forehead
mpuno · nose
mu- (1) · him/her – singular prefix or concord used for a human (noun class 1); see page 10
mu- (2) · singular prefix used for long or wooden things (noun class 3)
mu- (3) · in – locative prefix (page 16)
muβuyu · baobab tree
muchila · tail, follower (slang)
muchopo · barbecued meat ("chop")
mudala · sir (respectful term of address), father (slang)
mudima · darkness
mufana · younger sibling
mugodi · pit, hole, well
muja · in there (page 16)
mukame · polo neck
mukati · inside
mukazi · woman
mukolomino · uvula (at back of throat)
mukombo · navel
mukosi · neck
mukule · corn rows (hair style)
mukulu · older sibling

mukuyu · fig tree
mukwapu · whip
mulandu · dispute, legal case
mulaini · line
mulendo · guest
mulilo · fire
mulomo · lip, beak (of bird)
Mulungu · God
mumala · stomach
mumana · river
mumazulo · evening
mumbali · side
mumwamba · high
munda · field
mundikundiku · hiccups
munga · thorn, fish bone
munkoyo · a maize drink
muno · in here (page 16)
muntu · person
munyamata · boy
munza- · friend (page 14)
munzi · village
mupando · chair
mupelu · swing
mupongozi · son-in-law, daughter-in-law (respectful: *ßapongozi*)
mupundu · twin
musale · sugar cane
musana · back (of body)
museßo · road
mushe · good, well
musikana · girl
musonko · tax
muspikili · nail (for construction)
mutanda · crucifix
mutendere · peace

mutenge · roof
mutengo (flat tone) · price
mutengo (rising & falling tone) · tree
mutiko · cooking stick
mutima · heart
mutu · head
mutundu · type, kind of thing, tribe
muzimai · mother (respectful: *ßamai*)
muzimu · spirit, soul
muzukulu · grandchild
muzungu · white person
muzyu · root
-mva, -mvela · hear, feel, listen
-mvelela · listen seriously
-mvesa · understand
mvula · rain
mwa · inside of, in the manner of (page 14)
-mwa · drink
mwala · stone
mwamene · in the place which, in the manner which (page 15)
mwamuna · man
mwamusanga · easily
mwana · child
mwati · you said... (page 30)
mwayi · luck
mweka · by yourselves (page 25)
mwenze · you were (page 21)
mweve · in there (page 26)
mwezi · moon
mwinangu · in another place (page 26)
mwine · owner
-myanguta · lick

na · and, with
nacho, nako · with it
-nama · tell a lie
namba · number
-namizila · accuse
-nana · be wet
nanga · question marker (page 25)
nao · with it (page 26)
nati · I said... (page 30)
nato, navo · with them (page 26)
naye, nayeve · with him/her (page 25)
nayo · with it, with them (page 26)
nazo · with them (page 26)
nchisa · nest
nchito · work, job
ndaβa · because, why
ndalama · money
ndani? · who? (page 25)
ndazo · hat (slang)
ndeke · aeroplane
ndeo · fight
ndevu · beard
ndimwe, ndiwe · you are (page 24)
ndine · I am (page 24)
ndise · we are (page 24)
ndiye · he/she is, they are (page 24)
ndoβo · hook
neka · by myself (page 25)
nenze · I was (page 21)
-ng'amba · tear
-ng'ambika · be torn
ng'anga · witchdoctor
ngati · if, when (page 30)
-ngati? · how many? (page 25)
-ngena · enter, go in, set (sun)

-ngenesa · put in, score (goal)
ngoma · drum (instrument)
ng'ombe · cow, cattle
-ng'ung'uzila · mutter
-ngweleβela · be clear, transparent
ng'wena · crocodile
ni- · is, are (page 24)
ni- · I, me (subject/object prefix, page 19)
njala (flat tone) · fingernail, claw
njala (rising tone) · hunger
njanji · railway
njila · path, way
njinga · bicycle
njoka · snake
njoka ya mumala · intestinal worm
njota · thirst
njovu · elephant
-nkala · be, become, sit, stay (page 24)
nkalamu · lion
nkanda · skin
nkanga · guinea fowl
nkata · head pad (for carrying things)
nkokola · knee
nkoli · walking stick
nkoloko · clock
nkondo · war
nkongole · debt
nkonono · snail
nkote · old person
nkowa · egret, heron
nkuku · chicken
nkumba · pig
nkunda · dove
nkuni · wood
no- · shortening of **naku-** (page 30)

nsanya · bed bugs
nsapato · shoes
nsele · seed
nsengo · horn
nshaβa · groundnuts
nsima · nshima (cooked maize meal)
nsimbi · piece of metal, iron, car part
nsiye · eyelashes, eyebrows
nsalamu · token given during marriage negotiations
nsomba · fish
ntambi · tradition
ntambo · rope
ntanzi · health
ntawi · time
ntete · a small grasshopper
ntongo · lump of nshima (rolled in fingers)
ntoyo · Bambara groundnut
-nunka · smell (bad)
-nunkila · smell nice
-nya · defecate
nyakapelele · tiny flying ants
nyama · animal, meat
-nyamuka · stand up
-nyamula · carry, lift
-nyang'anya · move, shake
nyansi · bottom, underside
-nyaula · scratch
-nyaya · swim
nyele · sexual desire
nyelele · ant
nyeleti · needle
-nyeleza · be itchy
nyemba · beans
-nyenga · deceive, have sex

nyimbo · song
nyoni · bird
-nyonka · suckle (baby)
-nyonsha · breastfeed (give milk)
-nyowani · be new
nyumba · house
-nyumika · dry out
nzelu · wisdom, intelligence, mind
nzimu · bee
-nzuna · be sweet

o- · one who (page 15)
-ocha · roast, burn
odi · hello? (when entering a building)
-odila · knock/shout to enter
-ola · rot, be rotten
olo · or
-ona · see
-onela · care for, look after
-onesa · show, reveal
-onesesa · make sure
-ongoka · straight
-ononga · spoil, damage
-onongeka · be damaged
onse · all (page 26)
opusa · idiot, fool
osa- · don't (prohibition, page 28)

pa- · on, at (locative prefix, page 16)
pachifuβa · chest (body part)
pafupi · nearby
paja · there (page 16)
pakati · middle
-paking'a (1) · pack
-paking'a (2) · park (car)

pala · bald head
-pala · peel (with knife)
-palana · be similar
pambali · edge
pambuyo · before
pamene · when, while, at the place which (page 15)
pamenso · face
pamozi · together
pampa · be crowded
pamukosi · throat
pamwamba · up, above
panali panali · once upon a time
-panga · make, invent
pang'ono · a little
pang'ono-pang'ono · slowly
-panisha · punish
panja · outside
pano · here (page 16)
pansi · down, on the ground
pantawi ya · during, while
-papa · carry (on back), give birth
-papata · plead
papiko · wing
-pasa · give
patali · far away
pati? · where? (page 25)
-patula · part one's hair
-paya · kill
-peleka · hand over
-pelekeza · escort
-peluka · hang, swing on
-pema · breathe
-pempa · ask for, borrow
-pempela · pray
pempelo · prayer

penangu · somewhere else (page 26)
-penda · count
pene · when, while
-penta · paint
-pepa · inhale
pepe · feather
-pepeta · winnow
-pepuka · be lightweight
peve · there, at that place (page 26)
pewa · shoulder
-peza · find
-piβa · sweat
-pika · cook
pikicha · picture
-pilikisha · chase
-pima · measure
-pindamuka, -pindamula · turn round, turn over
pindu · value
-pipa · wipe one's bottom
-pisha · chase away
-pita · go, pass
-pitiliza · go on, continue
-pokelela · receive, get
-pola, -polesa · heal
-pomba · wind, twist
-pombana · be wound
pompi · tap, pump
-pombosoka · be unwound
-pombosola · unwind
-pompoloka, -poncha · be flat (tyre)
ponse · everywhere (page 26)
-ponya · throw
-ponyongola · bend, twist
poreji · porridge
-posha · greet

poto · pot
-pukuta · wipe, dry
pulanga · plank
-pulumusa · save, rescue
-pumula · rest, relax
-punda · shout
-punzila · learn
punzilo · lesson
-punzisa · teach
-pusa · be stupid, foolish
pusi · cat
-pwalala · be dim-witted
pwando · celebration, feast
-pwanya · smash, crush
-pwanyika · be smashed, crushed
pwele · bulbul (a bird)
-pya · be hot, cooked, ripe
-pyanga · sweep
-pyesa · heat up, ripen, be overcooked

-sa- · not (negative marker, page 20)
-sakila · search, look for
-sakula · comb
-sala · remain
saladi · cooking oil
-salangana · be scattered
-salanganya · scatter
-samalila · look after
-samba · bathe
-samila · lean
-samwa · be excited about
sando · hammer
sanga · forest
-sanika · shine, be bright
-sanka · choose

-sankaniza · mix up
-sashila · add groundnuts
-sauka · be poor
-sebanya · embarrass
-sebanyika · be embarrassed
-seβenzesa · use
sefa · sieve
-segula · open
-seka · laugh, laugh at
-sekelela · smile
-sekesa · have fun
-seluka · descend, disembark
-sema · carve
sembe · should have, would have (page 22)
-sensela · be loose, not fit well
shamwali · 'friend'
-shanga · plant (v.)
shawelo · shawl
-sheta · chew
shiβukombe · advisor to the groom in the process of marriage
-shimika · explain, describe
-shinda · wipe one's bottom
-shishita · be dim-witted
-shoka · burn, scorch
-shuβa · peel (e.g. banana)
-shula · fart
-shunshana · argue
-shupa · bother, trouble (v.)
-shuta · shoot
si- · not (negative marker, page 20)
siku · day
sikulu · school
-sila · end
-siliza · finish, complete

-*simikiza* · be sure
sisi · hair
-*siya* · leave, go away
-*siyana* · differ
-*siyanisa* · compare
-*soβa* · be lost, missing
-*soβela* · play
-*soβesa* · lose
-*sokoneza* · do wrong
-*sonjelela* · peek at
-*sonta* · point at
sontwa · big green grasshopper
-*sonyeza* · show, point at
sopo · soap
-*suka* · wash, brush (teeth)
-*sukuluza* · rinse
-*sunga* · care for
-*sungunuka* · be melted
-*sungunula* · melt
-*sunsha* · shake one's bottom
-*sunta* · limp
supuni · spoon

-*taβa* · run away, escape
-*taβila* · run to
-*taila* · disrespect a friend (slang)
-*takata* · hand over angrily
tako · buttock
-*tali* · long, tall, far
-*tamanga* · run
-*tamba* · watch
-*tandala, -tandalila* · visit
-*tandiza* · help
tandizo · help
-*tantauza* · mean, signify

-*tasha* · thank
tati · we said... (page 30)
-*tatu* · three (page 13)
-*tauka* · cross over
tauni · town, city
-*taya* · throw away
teβela · cloth nappy/diaper
-*teβeta* · put on a feast for a husband
-*teka* · be soft
teka · by ourselves (page 25)
-*telela* · be slippery, smooth
-*teleleka* · slip
-*tema* · chop, throw missile
-*tembenuka* · turn oneself around, be born again
-*tenga* · take
tenze · we were (page 21)
tepo · leaf
-*teya* · play (game), set a trap
ti- · we, us (subject/object prefix, page 19)
-*tila* · pour
-*tilila* · water (a plant)
-*tinika* · press
tobwa · a drink made from millet
-*tomola* · name (v.)
-*tonja* · gossip
tonje · cotton wool
tonse · all, all of us (page 25)
-*tota* · clap hands
tu- · little – plural prefix used for small things (noun class 13); corresponding singular forms begin with *ka-*; see page 10
-*tuβa* · be clean, bright
-*tukwana* · insult
-*tula* · break open, leak
tuleza · thunder, lightning

-tulika · broken open, leaky
tulo · sleep (n.)
-tulula · have diarrhoea
-tuma (1) · send, call
-tuma (2) · be warm
-tumisa · warm up
tumba · pocket
-tunda · urinate
-tunga · sew, weave, knit
-tunta · beat (heart)
-tunya · spit
tupi · body
tute · cassava
-tutuma · shiver
-twa (1) · pound
-twa (2) · be sharp
twa · of, belonging to (page 14)
tweve · them (page 26)
-twika · carry on one's head
twina, twinangu · some of them, others (page 26)
-twinga · poke, prick
-tyakula · stir/beat nshima
-tyoka · be broken, snapped
-tyola · break, snap

u- (1) · prefix used for certain abstract / mass nouns (noun class 14); see page 10
u- (2) · you (subject prefix, page 19)
uchi · honey
-uka · wake up
uko, uku · there, here (page 16)
ulemu · respect
ulendo · journey, trip
ulesi · boredom, laziness
-ulula · reveal

-umba · mould (into shape)
umfwiti · witchcraft
umo, umu · in there (page 16)
umoyo · life, health
unga · mealie meal (maize flour)
upuβa · foolishness
-usha · wake someone
usiku · night
uti? · which one?, who? (page 29)
utu · this (page 16)
-uza · tell
uyu · this (page 16)

va · of, belonging to, about (page 14)
-vala · block, shut, stop up, dress, put on clothes
-valika · dress someone
vamene, ve · those which (page 15)
veve · them (page 26)
vi- · plural prefix or concord used for 'things', particularly big or bad things (noun class 8); corresponding singular forms begin with *chi-*; see page 10
vikuti · hair twisted into spikes
-vimba · swell
-vina · dance
vina, vinangu · some of them, others (page 26)
-vipanga · pretend, role play
viponshi · gums (in mouth)
visashi · groundnut paste
viti? · which ones? (page 29)
vo- · those which (page 15)
-vomekeza · agree
-vomeleza · allow
vonse · all, everything (page 26)

-vota · vote (v.)
-vula · open, undress, take off clothes
-vundika · ripen (artificially)
-vundula · stir
-vununkula · uncover
-vuta · bother, trouble (v.)
-vutika · be bothered, troubled
vuto · trouble (n.), problem
vuzi · pubic hair

wa · of, belonging to (page 14)
-wala, -waling'a · worry (v.)
wamene · one who (page 15)
wamizana · interesting
-wamya · tidy, make nice
wanchito · servant, worker
wapamulumo · person who gossips
-washa · wash
wati · you said... (page 30)
weka · by yourself (page 25)
wenze · you were (page 21)
weve · it (page 26)
-wina · win
wina, winangu · another, one of you, another of you (page 25)

ya- · they, them – concord used for plural nouns in class 6; see page 10
ya · of, belonging to (page 14)
-yaka · alight, switched on
-yamba · start
-yambana · quarrel
-yambata · cover (with sheet)
-yambula · catch (disease)
-yamika · give thanks, give praise
yamene · that, which (page 15)

-yangana · look
-yanganila · look after
yangati? · how many? (page 25)
-yanika · hang up
-yanka · answer
-yasha · light, switch on
yati? · which ones? (page 29)
-yaula · yawn
-yembekeza · wait
yenangu · some of them, others (page 26)
-yenda · go
-yendela pa · ride on
-yendesa · hurry
-yentyemula · sneeze
-yenza · drive
-yesa · try
yeve · it, them (page 26)
-yewa · miss (regret absence)
-yimba · sing
-yina · be fat
yobali · gangster-style youth, chav
-yofya · frighten
-yonda · lean
-yondoloka, -yondolola · stretch, straighten
yonse · all (page 26)
-yopa · frightened
-yuma · dry

za · of, belonging to (page 14)
zeve · them (page 26)
-zezeleka · lose balance
zi- · it – concord used for plural nouns in class 4 or 10; see page 10
-ziβa · know

ziβa · breast
-ziβika · be familiar
-ziβisa · introduce
-zibuntula · trip
zii · quiet, 'cool' (slang)
ziko · country, world
zikomo · 'thank you'
-zima · be extinguished, switched off
-zimvesa · be proud
-zimya · extinguish, switch off
zina (1) · name
zina (2), *zinangu* · some of them, others (page 26)
zingati? · how many?, how much? (page 25)
ziti? · which ones? (page 29)
-zizila · be cold
-zola · rub, apply lotion
-zonda · hate
zonse · all (page 26)
zoona · truth, truly
zuβa · sun
-zula · be full
-zulisa · fill up
-zunguluka · go round

Printed in Germany
by Amazon Distribution
GmbH, Leipzig